WISDOM'S
CALL

WISDOM'S CALL

100 MEDITATIONS *for a* LIFE *in* CHRIST

K. A. ELLIS

MOODY PUBLISHERS

CHICAGO

Scripture quotations, unless otherwise marked, have been taken from the Christian
Standard Bible®, Copyright © 2017 by Holman Bible Publishers. Used by permission.
Christian Standard Bible® and CSB® are federally registered trademarks of Holman Bi-
ble Publishers.

Scripture quotations marked (ESV) are from the ESV® Bible (The Holy Bible, English
Standard Version®), copyright © 2001 by Crossway, a publishing ministry of Good
News Publishers. Used by permission. All rights reserved. The ESV text may not be
quoted in any publication made available to the public by a Creative Commons license.
The ESV may not be translated in whole or in part into any other language.

Scripture quotations marked (NLT) are taken from the Holy Bible, New Living Transla-
tion, copyright ©1996, 2004, 2015 by Tyndale House Foundation. Used by permission
of Tyndale House Publishers, Carol Stream, Illinois 60188. All rights reserved.

All emphasis in Scripture has been added.

Portions of Meditations 4, 5, 6, 7, 10, and the epilogue first appeared in K. A. Ellis, "Everybody Plays the Fool: Discipling Women from Foolishness to Wisdom," in Beyond the
Roles: A Biblical Foundation for Women and Ministry, ed. Melanie Cogdill (Lawrencev-
ille, GA: PCA Committee on Discipleship Ministries, 2019). Portions of Meditations
71, 72, 74–77 are from a Gospel Coalition podcast with the author. A portion of #96
was in urbanfaith.com/author/karen-angela-ellis/.

Published in association with Don Gates, THE GATES GROUP, www-the-gates-
group.com.

Edited by Pamela Joy Pugh
Interior design: Kaylee Dunn
Cover design and illustration: Kaylee Dunn
Cover texture of wavy lines copyright © 2023 by rawpixel.com/Freepik.com. All rights
reserved.

ISBN: 978-0-8024-2512-6

Originally delivered by fleets of horse-drawn wagons, the affordable paperbacks from
D. L. Moody's publishing house resourced the church and served everyday people.
Now, after more than 125 years of publishing and ministry, Moody Publishers' mission
remains the same—even if our delivery systems have changed a bit. For more information on other books (and resources) created from a biblical perspective, go to www
.moodypublishers.com or write to:

Moody Publishers
820 N. LaSalle Boulevard
Chicago, IL 60610

1 3 5 7 9 10 8 6 4 2

Printed in the United States of America

For Dorothy Bennett and Grace Odums,
whose wisdom from Christ was first pure,
then peaceable, gentle, open to reason, full of mercy
and good fruits, impartial and sincere;
I'll see you both in glory.

CONTENTS

ON WISDOM'S THRESHOLD

You've chosen a devotional on wisdom . . . you must have heard her calling out to you.

"Momma don't raise no fools" was a common expression in our household. Papa didn't either. Most parents, whether they follow the ways of Christ or not, don't want their children to be involved in foolishness, or know the pain that foolishness brings.

I haven't come to write about wisdom because I am wise; I am not. Too often I have been the very opposite, living foolishly and destructively. However, somewhere along the way Wisdom's call pricked my conscience as I grew tired of hurting those around me, and even of hurting myself with the consequences of my choices.

Wisdom calls, and I come to her door like a beggar drawn to the gates of the wealthy.

Solomon, who asked God for wisdom and who is credited with many (but not all) of the wisdom sayings we find in the book of Proverbs, was regarded by the people of his day as the wisest man in the world. His reputation for wisdom spread so far and wide in the ancient world that an African queen from Sheba traveled for miles upon miles with complete retinue in tow to grapple over the life-defining concerns and issues of her people. She was not seeking Solomon, but wisdom for herself to govern and rule her people well, perhaps even for personal concerns of her own. Being known as a "wise person" seemed to be an aspirational good, a commodity whose fame travels well.

For some strange reason, I always thought that if I asked God for wisdom, He would just supernaturally impart it as He did for Solomon.

It was when I found myself curled up in a ball on the bed with tears streaming down my face over an impossible dilemma that I realized God works out wisdom for us in real time by giving us His Word, His Holy Spirit, and then real-life situations where we can exercise our muscles of discernment. This is how He grows us in the faith and knowledge of life, according to His original garden plan.

Yet Scripture reveals that not even Solomon was supernaturally zapped with an impartation of wisdom. One of Solomon's first assignments to demonstrate wisdom was a messy, literally life-and-death case: two women disputing over the cover-up of a seemingly accidental infanticide, with a side of kidnapping added to the charges (1 Kings 3:16–27). Dealing with the two women arguing required listening, inquiry, prayer, consultation with parties involved, and then prayer for... you guessed it, wisdom. Wisdom to know right from wrong, to know life from death, to discern hearts and motivations.

God has made it so that His universe and its inhabitants are guided by two primary principles: wisdom brings freedom and life, folly brings destruction and death.

Every major choice (and even some minor ones!) made by any of our spiritual ancestors in the Bible can be seen as a choice between God or self, life or death, freedom or bondage, wisdom or folly. Proverbs in particular belongs to a type of writing that is set for the purpose of developing wisdom in those curious enough to seek her out to develop moral skill and mental acumen; to move beyond acquiring information and being smart, to becoming disciplined, gaining insight into human nature, to become a just and fair person, to listen to God's way of doing things, and add to the knowledge He has so willingly poured out from Himself onto His creation.

Beyond Proverbs, however, the whole of Scripture carries that same intention to help mankind live well in a fallen world. Sometimes Scripture teaches us directly about particular life situations, and at other times it provides insight and direction into the truths of eternal certainty. And sometimes it does both! From Genesis to Revelation, Scripture reveals God's plan for human beings. It tells the stories of those who answered Wisdom's call and sought God's ways above their own, as well as the stories of those who deliberately chose Folly's house of pain.

Scripture even tells the stories of spiritual ancestors who jumped between the two houses in the same lifetime.

My prayer is these meditations will encourage a lifetime of eager desire to dwell in Wisdom's house—the house of shalom, life, comfort, endurance, and justice deep in our hearts, and that we'll experience together the richness of our communion with God that flows out to others and to all of God's creation.

Wisdom has called us, Friend. Come on into this house and come to stay . . . adventure awaits.

1

WHO IS WISE?

Perhaps the most famous of the wisdom books in the Bible is Proverbs. It tells us at its outset why it exists:

For learning wisdom and discipline;
for understanding insightful sayings;
for receiving prudent instruction
in righteousness, justice, and integrity;
for teaching shrewdness to the inexperienced,
knowledge and discretion to a young man—
let a wise person listen and increase learning,
and let a discerning person obtain guidance—
for understanding a proverb or a parable,
the words of the wise, and their riddles.
(Prov. 1:2–7)

Life is confusing and at times, profoundly disappointing. If God hadn't provided His Word and the Holy Spirit to guide us into all wisdom and joy, we would most certainly be people of absolute despair, with the pain of the world obscuring its joys and triumphs.

Once we gather some years and a bit of grey hair at the temple, we realize that some of life's difficulties were the result of suffering the consequence of our own choices. At times those choices were made from ignorance, at other times selfishly motivated, and still at other times completely against the counsel of those who already knew the briar-covered path and had the scars to prove it.

Yet there are some who have come through this pilgrim's journey as if it were a nomadic adventure—hard-won wisdom that produces joy in knowing what is the right thing in the worst situations. Imagine a nomadic people group who have always lived off the land. Their children are told as they walk along where the hazards are. In the savanna, death lurks in the tall grass where the lions hide; in the tundra, the danger lies in crossing the thin ice. In each case, those who are journeying pass on vital, life-saving information.

We call these people wise.

Some who have not traveled the path reject their wisdom and grow more foolish with each passing year, only wishing to satisfy themselves. The old people used to say there's no fool like an old fool, battle-scarred and never learning. Old on the outside, but children within. We all know people who've grown old yet never learned that the low grass provides clearer vision, that a whole community can cross on thicker ice. Moreover, the foolish do not only hurt themselves, since we never sin in a vacuum; our foolish choices always affect others because we are a connected, communal people made to either bless or curse after the fashion of our triune, promise-keeping Creator.

These people, we call fools.

It's at the humble threshold of wisdom and life that we leave folly behind, where we move from haphazard to disciplined and from ignorant to understanding, able to receive from those who are elder-wise, trading shrewdness for inexperience, and pursue righteous, just, and holy living that respects our own dignity and the dignity of others.

And be prepared for the words of the wise in riddles: they are vexing and fun, much better lived than told.

A HOUSE IS
NOT A HOME

What transforms a house into a home? Any structure can be a house, but it's the elements within—especially the people—and what qualities they bring that make it a home. I've noticed that even the most beautifully appointed home can feel terribly hollow if the occupants I love are not there. Of course, in a busy home I enjoy the stillness and the quiet, but also because of the lingering memories of the occupants who have filled the rooms and my heart with their peace.

Some of our spiritual ancestors sang from the depths of their souls, toil, and harsh labor: "I've got a home in glory land that outshines the sun."[1] They sang of the Home that Christ Himself has prepared—for the construction is already done, and the keys secured the moment He emerged from the grave to lead us captives to the door. He tells us that His Home has many rooms, space for all He has gathered in. In His Home, there is pleasant work. The fragrances of perfect peace and purpose rise from every corner to bless our glorified senses. The fragrance of life reigns because He is there—the chief architect of the structure that was set stone upon stone, filling it with the safety and fulfillment of His people in mind.

Look around. The architect has set glimpses of this glorious Home all around for us to discover, for our delight. The psalmist saw these homes of peace and order all around him, parting tree limbs and peering into the homes of God's tiniest creatures nestled between branches. God fashions homes for even the sparrow and the swallow, "a nest for herself where she places her young . . . near your altars" (Ps. 84:3). So safe are these little ones that they trust their young—that is, their future and their hope—to Him.

---

1. "I've Got a Home in Glory Land," https://hymnary.org/text/ive_got_a_home_in_glory_land.

How content are the psalmist's swallow and sparrow, more secure than in the palm of any human hand. Safe. Nestled. Protected and watched over by the Creator Himself, who reminds us today that we have a home in glory land that outshines the sun.

And as the psalmist meditates on his promised place of shalom, like Adam he names it aptly . . . he calls it *lovely*.

So it is with Wisdom's house.

How lovely is your dwelling place,
LORD of Armies.
I long and yearn
for the courts of the LORD;
my heart and flesh cry out for the living God.

Even a sparrow finds a home,
and a swallow, a nest for herself
where she places her young—
near your altars, LORD of Armies
my King and my God.
How happy are those who reside in your house,
who praise you continually.
(Ps. 84:1–4)

3

THE WORLD RUNS
ON WISDOM

The LORD founded the earth by wisdom
and established the heavens by understanding.
By his knowledge the watery depths broke open,
and the clouds dripped with dew.

PROVERBS 3:19–20

The psalmist marvels aloud at creation around him: Christ has
created everything seen and unseen. We live in an ordered, intricately interdependent yet harmonious universe.

Even though our age is one of cynicism, even pessimism, every one
of us still feels our breath catch at the sight of a shooting star, or when
the curtain of the northern lights descends and dances, or as we survey
the wonder of tiny nails, eyebrows, and toes of a fresh, newborn babe.

The foundation of this ordered world stands so firm with the imprint of its Creator's wisdom that even though the destructive folly of
Satan would mar its beauty and introduce decay, the principles of physics still define and drive it.

We see numerous affirmations scattered throughout Scripture that
Christ is the wisdom on which our world rests. These assurances exist
as our treasure, like iridescent pearls scattered across the page. The letter to the Colossians declares that Christ is the Creator of all things in
the universe (Col. 1:16), and the Corinthian epistle likewise draws on
Solomon's treasury with this truth: Christ Himself is our wisdom, and
our way of understanding the world (1 Cor. 1:16–31).

Even though it is a fallen beauty, it is a majestic beauty still, with human beings as creation's pinnacle: a marvel of divine engineering, living,
sentient machines that run independently and are capable of worship,

living beings with souls, each possessing a curious battery called a heart that runs without a plug, and cease at the Creator's determining.

We run alive, with the breath of our Creator in our lungs.

And yet there are terrible things marring the beauty of all that is made—people, flora, fauna alike. Nothing has escaped the effects of the fall.

Scripture tells us that if we get wisdom, understanding follows. Apart from Christ, our wisdom—what we are able to know and do, anything that builds life—is an act of His grace. Proverbs tells us more about wisdom. The book tells us that the Lord, who is Wisdom Himself, used the innate qualities of wisdom to lay the earth's foundation. In truth, the Creator is why the world, for all its brokenness and destruction, still makes sense and hangs together as a whole, since wisdom was the foundation of the cosmos design. Seasons still color our landscapes; spring still predictably follows winter in the places where it should.

Day follows night, and the sun hangs in the sky and marks our time. Animals, fish, and fowl remain fed and true to their nature. Kingdoms still rise and fall, and here is humanity in the middle of it all, despite the fallen nature of the world as we know it . . . His world crafted by wisdom, founded on wisdom, still sings.

CHRIST IS
OUR WISDOM

Christ is the power of God and the wisdom of God. . . . It is from
[God] that you are in Christ Jesus, who became wisdom from God
for us—our righteousness, sanctification, and redemption.

1 CORINTHIANS 1:24, 30

Paul teaches in his letter to Corinth that the uncreated Christ Himself is our wisdom.

Yes, Wisdom is a person—the person of Christ, the Creator of all things. His wise fingerprints are upon us, His breath of life is inside us, and His image covers us inside and out. Wisdom's imprint on us is a part of God's garden package. By dwelling with wisdom in the person of Christ, by whom, in whom, and through whom all things were made, our first parents relied on Him to explain their world. Having unhindered communion with the triune God in some form while they lived in the garden, they were to pattern themselves after His image by understanding the world through His eyes.

While the Bible speaks of Wisdom as a person, it also speaks of wisdom as a benefit to life, created by Christ at the foundation of the world. Proverbs 8 tells us that the Lord brought wisdom forth as the first of His works, before His deeds of old, appointed before eternity, before the world began (see vv. 22–23). Before the "Let us makes" of Genesis 1, even before the "Let there bes," Wisdom was.

Let's continue to think of Wisdom both as a person (Christ), and as an asset created by that person . . . a byproduct of the source of all wisdom, if you will.

Wisdom and truth are part of the testament to the richness of that image of God bestowed on humankind that separates us from the animals. (I hesitate to say it's the whole, because no library could exhaust the contents of the image of God.) But we cannot deny that *wisdom the life-force* was imparted to man by *Wisdom the Person*, when Christ breathed life into mankind and he became a living, breathing soul contained in a body.

Imagine that first intaking of breath . . . the first breath of life, how thrilling it must have been for Creator and creature, the tender exchange of life-giving, life-making air, billowing into the lungs from Life Himself.

We sing then with wisdom and amazement of the psalmist:

> When I observe your heavens,
> the work of your fingers,
> the moon and the stars,
> which you set in place,
> what is a human being that you remember him,
> a son of man that you look after him?
> You made him little less than God
> and crowned him with glory and honor.
> You made him ruler over the works of your hands;
> you put everything under his feet.
> (Ps. 8:3–7)

WISDOM'S STAMP

The exact substance of wisdom is difficult to grasp hold of, because that substance is God Himself. Yet we can understand wisdom's substance by its expressions and also by its effects, which God has given us as visual aids.

One tangible expression of wisdom is the ordered universe in which we live. Though we know it now as a fallen world with brokenness shot through it, it remains beautiful and ordered and held together by His will and power. Matthew Henry, still highly regarded after three centuries for his biblical commentary, taught us that divine revelation is the word and wisdom of God, that the Redeemer is the eternal Word, and wisdom the Logos. So wisdom contains the power, understanding, and knowledge of the Trinity.

> Then God said, "Let us make man in our image, according to our likeness. They will rule the fish of the sea, the birds of the sky, the livestock, the whole earth, and the creatures that crawl on the earth."
>
> So God created man
> in his own image;
> he created him in the image of God;
> he created them male and female.
> (Gen. 1:26–27)

Adam first out of the dust, and Eve next out of his side. Ironically, among all the non-human creatures from which God made many couples, man is the only one where He fashioned two out of one. The man *and* the woman seem to be a physical extension of the relational intimacy of the Trinity's creative force. By the handiwork of the interconnected yet distinct Three come an interconnected but distinct One.

Wisdom's imprint on the first people is also a trinity of sorts: (1) *in knowledge*, their ability to see divine things clearly and truly, and there were no errors or mistakes in their knowledge; (2) *in righteousness*, in that the first couple's will complied readily and universally with the will of God without reluctance or resistance; and (3) *in true holiness* (Eph. 4:24; Col. 3:10; Eccl. 7:29).

This imprint of wisdom defines the byproduct we call shalom. The first people of God enjoyed complex, interwoven relationships and affection among all the involved parties. They knew harmony with the rest of creation, as well as trust, communion, identity, security, and a lack of want.

This shalom was marked by three distinct blessings: presence, where God dwelt with man; property in a newly fashioned heaven and earth; and peace, as they lived in harmony with each other and the world around them. The garden, under Christ-directed shalom, was created to be a sanctuary and protected place.

Wisdom is then, at the very least, a window into the image of God. It is a part of the "very good" of garden life, a part of the situation that was most conducive to human flourishing. Throughout Proverbs and the rest of Scripture, Christ's breath of life, of wisdom, of presence-dwelling and shalom, continues to be a life-giving force wherever it is found.

This picture gives us a scriptural definition for flourishing: the shalom of dwelling with the Creator, with no hindrances or obstacles to understanding His world, His intentions, and His purposes through His eyes. Shalom—or flourishing—is dwelling with Wisdom Himself, and it is directly tied to obedience to the source of wisdom. Shalom was never intended as a goal to be obtained; it's not something humans can strive for or can even create. Though we create in God's image by His mercy, our Creator stands as the only One who can wisely shape a world perfectly suited to our hopes, needs, and even our godly desires.

6

THIS NEW THING
CALLED FEAR

Satan, the author of folly and destruction, ruined himself by attempting to be like the Most High: "How you are fallen from heaven, O Day Star, son of Dawn! How you are cut down to the ground, who laid the nations low! You said in your heart, 'I will ascend to heaven; above the stars of God I will set my throne on high; I will sit on the mount of assembly in the far reaches of the north; I will ascend above the heights of the clouds; I will make myself like the Most High'" (Isa. 14:12–14 ESV). This was ambition at its loftiest and its most foolish, to attempt an act that could never be attained.

The one who could not bear to dwell with the Prince of Peace cozied up to the woman and persuaded her that the tree of the knowledge of good and evil, which had been forbidden by God, "was good for food, and that it was a delight to the eyes, *and that the tree was to be desired to make one wise,* [so] she took of its fruit and ate, and she also gave some to her husband who was with her, and he ate" (Gen. 3:6 ESV).

He called her to Folly's side, and how ironic that wisdom is included in the deception! The first people were already wise, since they walked and dwelt with Wisdom Himself. Wisdom was the first and natural orientation of our parents in the garden. But they chose instead to dwell with foolishness, and we as their children dwell with foolishness. Wisdom and Truth are two sides of the same coin, while Foolishness and Lies are also two sides of the same coin.

The result of the abandonment of wisdom, obedience, and shalom is reported in Romans 1:

For although they knew God, they did not honor him as God or give thanks to him, but they became futile in their thinking, and their foolish hearts were darkened. Claiming to be wise, they became fools, and exchanged the glory of the immortal God for images resembling mortal man and birds and animals and creeping things. (vv. 21–23 ESV)

The depth of grief the first couple likely felt when peace with God was shattered can't be understated. They experienced an instantaneous transition from peace to chaos, knowing abject fear and shame, hiding because "I was afraid . . . I was naked."

What is this new thing I feel, called fear? What this new thing I sense, called nakedness? Imagine, these never-before-known emotions cascading down on their heads and into their hearts, after knowing only shalom.

7

LEAN ON ME

Our first parents knew wisdom through intimacy with Christ. When temptation and sin slithered into the garden, so came Folly—Wisdom's envious and unfortunate partner throughout Scripture.

They chose instead to dwell with folly and foolishness, and we as their children dwell with the foolishness of our own understanding of the world, apart from the One who created the world. Folly was not a part of the "very good" created order. It was forced upon the man and the woman by a hostile and deceitful enemy, hell-bent on frustrating the first couple's God-given shalom.

Wisdom's world of obedience was disfigured. Everything that made her a haven of rest and safety contorted into something grotesque, the product of fearsome rebellion.

In an instant, the lights dimmed a bit, the trees drooped, and creation uttered her first weighted groan. Relationship became brokenness, affection became resentment, trust turned to suspicion, unity morphed into discord, security decayed into danger, balance yielded to oppression, abundance evaporated into paucity. To echo Ophelia in Shakespeare's *Hamlet*, the sweet bells of harmony with creation became "jangled, out of tune and harsh."

Put another way, wisdom and truth brought them peace and harmony; folly and lies brought chaos and disorder.

As a result, the tuition for biblical wisdom ever since is now become astronomically high; we can take fire in our laps and experience the pain on our own flesh, or we can trace inquisitive fingers along the burn scars of others and ask, "What hurt you—was it your folly, or someone else's foolish flame that jumped on you?"

And then we listen for the wisdom. But however the knowledge of consequence comes, someone has paid the price to know what is good and what is not.

Imagine if our first parents had followed the old proverb, stitched and hung on many a wall for generations:

Trust in the Lord with all your heart, and do not lean on your own understanding. In all your ways acknowledge him, and he will make straight your paths. Be not wise on your own eyes; fear the Lord and turn from evil. It will be healing to your flesh and refreshment to your bones. (Prov. 3:5–8 esv)

Imagine if we better followed these wise words today!

WISDOM
LOVES LIFE

Who pays the price for becoming wise? If Folly had its own banking system, humanity would write checks on the overdrawn account of human wisdom.

Scripture tells us that wisdom is a high commodity in the open market of life, and often it comes at the expense of bills that our own folly racks up; we learn the cost of both by experience. Sometimes the education comes by ignorance, e.g., "I didn't know the stove was hot, but my blistering finger tells me it was so!" At other times, our curiosity drives our willingness to pay the price: "This stove has burned me before, so I know I can withstand the searing pain."

Proverbs 3 reminds us that to grasp wisdom is to take hold of one of the most valuable, even powerful, weapons in life. And of course, it is—for to grasp wisdom is to invite the mind of Christ Himself, the One who ordered the world and keeps it hanging together. To grasp Christ's mind for His creation is much more than understanding what is right and wrong; it is a return to the peace, knowledge, and shalom of the One who created the whole system of life. He has paid the tuition on our behalf and left us the record of His world in natural and special revelation. He has left His Spirit to guide us into all knowledge and wisdom to the place that our spiritual parents forsook:

> Happy is a man who finds wisdom
> and who acquires understanding,
> for she is more profitable than silver,
> and her revenue is better than gold.
> She is more precious than jewels;
> nothing you desire can equal her.

Long life is in her right hand;
in her left, riches and honor.
Her ways are pleasant,
and all her paths, peaceful.
She is a tree of life to those who embrace her,
and those who hold on to her are happy. (Prov. 3:13–18)

Wisdom beckons us with a full scholarship to her academy, bought and paid for by the Creator and the return to wisdom made possible through the blood-bought redemption of Christ. Christ, in the wisdom of the kind Creator, has given us His wisdom in the form of written Word, explaining the ordered workings of His universe.

Happiness and peace are the lifelong possession of the one who garners wisdom. Does this mean that unfortunate things, even destructive things, will never happen to the wise? Certainly not. No comfortable life is promised to the Christian, but rather trouble is promised; yet we are instructed to take heart in the midst of trouble because Wisdom Himself has overcome the world. He will hold the Christian together in peace, even when the world is falling apart.

WISDOM'S CALL

Many voices call out to us in the brief hours of a day. We receive phone calls from familiar voices, emails, texts, calls from our own hallways and from up the stairs of our homes. We are bombarded with ads that entice us to momentary pleasure at the expense of our pain, that one last meeting with the wrong person, or whichever drug of choice we find irresistible. These voices crowd in and echo with insistent and increasing volume, attempting to obscure Wisdom's voice if we do not take care. They know what we like, they know what we want.

Both modern and developing worlds provide an abundance of distractions calling for our time and attention, but it seems like more than ever before. Neurobiologists who specialize in the brain's functions and how it adapts to the world around us teach us that while our bodies experience both pain and pleasure in similar ways, our bodies are exhausted by balancing the dissonance between the two. Perhaps this is our Creator calling from inside His creation to discern between the fruit of wisdom and folly, and that our understanding the difference extends into, even begins in, our brains.

It's no wonder then, that Scripture instructs us to be transformed by the renewing of our minds (Rom. 12:2). Detaching from the distractions and calls of other voices intent on harm is a weighty task when they are everywhere, targeting us from a distance us like a hustler seeking a mark.

There are many human voices woven into the stories of the Bible; the voices of husbands directing wives and wives directing husbands, of rulers directing their people, of prophets speaking the words and will of God, of those treated unjustly crying out in the desert for recompense; voices persuading, condemning, upbraiding, and even encouraging us to draw near to the ultimate voice, such as that of John the Baptist crying in the wilderness to "make straight the way of the Lord."

The voice of Wisdom that commands and beckons us to come apart from those is distinct from all others; it beckons us to come, be refreshed, renewed, made alive, and live. This is the voice of the Shepherd, by whom His sheep are known. And so as all others fall away in this moment, we tune our voice to His:

> Doesn't wisdom call out?
> Doesn't understanding make her voice heard?
> At the heights overlooking the road,
> at the crossroads, she takes her stand.
> Beside the gates leading into the city,
> at the main entrance, she cries out:
> "People, I call out to you;
> my cry is to the children of Adam.
> Learn to be shrewd, you who are inexperienced;
> develop common sense, you who are foolish." (Prov. 8:1–5)

There is no shame in Wisdom's call. Wisdom wants not only to be heard, she wants to be seen. Wisdom calls to us as high and grand as a living statue, raised on the highest places, high atop a hill so that all may see who it is that is calling, and see who is flocking toward this voice of life.

Note here that the invitation is to everyone. All people are welcome at Wisdom's door, and that includes you and me. Shakespeare's sprite Puck famously said, "Lord, what fools these mortals be!" And this is us as well, for we are all under the foolishness of Adam after the fall.

The school of wisdom is the most inclusive and comprehensive educational plan known to mankind . . . it is also the most essential.

LADY WISDOM
SPEAKS

Proverbs 8 is a gift to all women who belong to the people of God. Because it is a gift to women of God, it is a gift to all the people of God, for in God's life-giving economy, what is good for one is good for all.

God presents Wisdom, and her opposing force Folly, in the feminine. The two women are the star players in this analogy of the grand choice of life.

In fact, God paints for us a picture of two women, living in two houses, serving two meals, with two communities, and based on two separate lives. Casting the two women feels like a literary absolution of the first woman's disobedience in the garden, where her mind, heart, body, and soul stood at the crossroads of life and death.

In painting the picture, He asks us to stand before the final word picture and bids us to ask questions: Which of these two houses is the dwelling that will lead to the shalom intended in that first garden shelter? Which one is the home that resulted in the first tempting bite that threw the world off-kilter?

As the Bible speaks of Lady Wisdom, our ears open to recognize the distinctive voice of personal Wisdom that's found as an abundant fountain in the second person of the Godhead. We hear that voice as the very voice of God cascading through His Word and works:

Listen, for I speak of noble things, and what my lips say is right.

For my mouth tells the truth, and wickedness is detestable to my lips.

All the words from my mouth are righteous; none of them are deceptive or perverse.

All of them are clear to the perceptive, and right to those who discover knowledge.

Accept my instruction instead of silver, and knowledge rather than pure gold.

For wisdom is better than jewels, and nothing desirable can equal it. (Prov. 8:6–11)

In this we find the echoes of Paul, and what we should all listen for and heed from our Shepherd's voice: "Finally brothers and sisters, whatever is true, whatever is honorable, whatever is just, whatever is pure, whatever is lovely, whatever is commendable—if there is any moral excellence and if there is anything praiseworthy—dwell on these things" (Phil. 4:8). The things that are the opposite of a righteous, noble nature and of truth are named—deceitfulness, wickedness, perversion of the created order—these do not belong in Wisdom's house and therefore we can neither dwell on them nor dwell with them. Nothing impure comes from the lips of the Shepherd, and nothing against His character will enter Wisdom's house. Not only will His distinctive voice be clear to those who seek Him, so will their understanding of His precepts.

Debates will continue throughout human history about the ownership and value of the world's finest and largest jewels worn in the crowns of earthly kings and queens. Yet even the commodities of the ages that have withstood the tests of war, tech, and time cannot eclipse the value of knowing this voice.

The world lusts after silver, gold, and precious diamonds and rubies, but they all pale in comparison to knowing and hungering after Wisdom's voice.

UNSHAKABLE
FOUNDATION

The house of Wisdom is unshakable because its foundation,
the King of kings, cannot be shaken.

I exalt you, my God the King,
and bless your name forever and ever.

PSALM 145:1

D avid must have loved singing this song. That it was David's song
of praise intimates that not only did he write it, but that he took
particular pleasure in it; it was his companion and comfort wherever he
went, perhaps even long before he was a king.

And this is so good to David's heart and ear—such a rich declaration—that David repeats and doubles down . . .

I will bless you every day;
I will praise your name forever and ever.
(Ps. 145:2)

There is no succession plan in this kingdom. This is a forever rule,
and it is not only David's duty to praise and extol the King's virtue as a
subject in the kingdom, it is his delight. Our praise shall have no end, because this kingdom shall have no end. If David can praise the name of his
King forever and ever, it is because the King will reign forever and ever.
Not even death can shake the house of Wisdom that King Jesus rules!

In the beginning was the Word, and the Word was with God, and
the Word was God. He was with God in the beginning. All things

were created through him, and apart from him not one thing was created that has been created. In him was life, and that life was the light of men. That light shines in the darkness, and yet the darkness did not overcome it. (John 1:1–5)

Christ has laid the kingdom to run on the foundation of His wisdom. He built the pillars that uphold the structure, and everything in His world runs on His power and knowledge; how He has set it to work for our good and His ultimate glory. Since He laid out its workings, He was the only one who could upset the natural physics of death. He is the only one who held the keys to upending and redeeming all of His creation for its intended purpose—to be the dwelling place for a King and His people.

When earthly kings and queens die, they stay dead. The whole world is a mausoleum of archeological digs and graves, memorials, tombs, cathedral sepulchres, and cemeteries full of kings and queens who died and did not resurrect. Their tombs are still full.

But we have a greater King whose tomb is empty! No succession plan is needed for a King who reigns from beginning to end. He will, forever, receive praise every eternal day for this marvelous, miraculous work of defying natural laws He Himself set in place.

This ruler of wisdom is impervious to destruction; so are His kingdom and we, His people. If we put ourselves in the psalmist's shoes, we should give glory to God every day and everywhere: in our solemn devotions, in our art, in our common conversation. If our hearts are full of God, then out of the abundance of our mouths will speak with reverence—with praise—on all occasions.

WISDOM'S
QUICKENING

Then Jesus, deeply moved again, came to the tomb. It was a cave, and a stone was lying against it. "Remove the stone," Jesus said.

Martha, the dead man's sister, told him, "Lord, there is already a stench because he has been dead four days."

Jesus said to her, "Didn't I tell you that if you believed you would see the glory of God?"

So they removed the stone. Then Jesus raised his eyes and said, "Father, I thank you that you heard me. I know that you always hear me, but because of the crowd standing here I said this, so that they may believe you sent me." After he said this, he shouted with a loud voice, "Lazarus, come out!" The dead man came out bound hand and foot with linen strips and with his face wrapped in a cloth. Jesus said to them, "Unwrap him and let him go." (John 11:38–44)

Lies we've believed about ourselves wrap around us like grave clothes. They swaddle us in a death grip, telling us we must live this false identity in a house of death and decay. Yet once we hear even the faintest echo of Wisdom's call, our eyes, once closed in death, pop open and interrogate our surroundings, and suddenly we want to live!

We look down at our grave clothes and smell their stench. All at once, we see what we once were and what we actually are. Wisdom's call has snatched our blinders and shown us the reality of the house of the dead.

But as it is, Christ has been raised from the dead, the first fruits of those who have fallen asleep. For since death came through a man, the resurrection of the dead also comes through a man. For just as in Adam all die, so also in Christ all will be made alive. (1 Cor. 15:20–22)

Once we come alive in the grave we've dug for ourselves, we cry to be lifted out. And when the Spirit opens our eyes, our grave will be empty, just like His.

No longer dead in Adam, we are now alive in Christ. He unbinds the grave clothes that hold us, and we come Home.

This is what it is to approach the threshold of Wisdom's house.

13

DRINK DEEP

You made him little less than God and
crowned him with glory and honor.
You made him ruler over the works of your hands;
you put everything under his feet:
all the sheep and oxen as well as the animals in the wild,
the birds of the sky and the fish of the sea that pass
through the currents of the seas.
LORD, our Lord, how magnificent is your name
throughout the earth!

PSALM 8:5–9

Our distinct way of knowing—of being able to not merely know
but to grow wise—is a part of the Creator's wisdom. The animals
may bring us their vivid personalities, express their intelligence and
reasoning, and even show affection toward us, but we are still different from them. Some can be trained, others can be domesticated and
tamed. All creation hunts, gathers, multiplies, chirps, whistles, swims,
moves via wings or on two feet or four. All creation worships the Creator, simply by doing what they were created to do. Though by man's
hand creation has been broken, all creation still worships obediently
by submitting to the ordered world established for them. Creatures are
even able to learn; but they cannot grow wise and apply their wisdom
in the way that human beings can. Despite their varied abilities, they
still live in the confined circle of their God-given instincts and drives.
We are different from them; Genesis tells us that we have God's image,
and they do not.

Man, in God's likeness, looks for meanings so that he can control
and direct his instinctive desires. It might be easier and more satisfying

to become animalistic and satisfy all our primal urges, but even as we do so we cannot escape God's imprint on us. Our consciences eventually will prick us, simply because we are human and possess consciences to be pricked with regret. Yes, we experience regret, and ponder the deeper things that are especially human, such as why, how, and for what purpose?

Though we are distinct from the animals, we are also distinct from God. We are fallen human beings who need wisdom; we need life and the illumination that come from the worship of God. One brother in Christ captures the differences this way:

> Even Christians, with a fuller revelation than Solomon had still cannot see the whole plan, though faith enables them to see that in everything God works for good to those who love him and are called according to his purpose. There is much we cannot understand, but our efforts at aiming for unsubstantial and ungodly ideals, and our efforts to straighten things out and supply what seems to be lacking will always lead to disappointment. We simply cannot break through our barriers between our wisdom and God's. If we could, he wouldn't be God. We are wholly dependent on God's great wisdom, and His increased knowledge.[1]

We will never cross over to own the fountain and source of wisdom; however, we are privileged to drink deeply from it.

And because we are human, drink deeply we must.

O what a magnificent Creator, to make from wisdom a gift of such distinctions!

---

1. Frank E. Gaebelein, ed., *The Expositor's Bible Commentary (Vol. 5): Psalms–Song of Songs* (Grand Rapids, MI: Regency Reference Library, 1991), 943–50.

WISDOM'S
BURDEN

I, the Teacher, have been king over Israel in Jerusalem. I applied my mind to examine and explore through wisdom all that is done under heaven. God has given people this miserable task to keep them occupied. I have seen all the things that are done under the sun and have found everything to be futile, a pursuit of the wind.

What is crooked cannot be straightened; what is lacking cannot be counted.

I said to myself, "See, I have amassed wisdom far beyond all those who were over Jerusalem before me, and my mind has thoroughly grasped wisdom and knowledge."

I applied my mind to know wisdom and knowledge, madness and folly;

I learned that this too is a pursuit of the wind.

For with much wisdom is much sorrow; as knowledge increases, grief increases. (Eccl. 1:12–18)

King Solomon—teacher, preacher, king—wrote a good amount of what we find in the wisdom books of our Scriptures. In truth, as we know, he is regarded by Scripture itself as the wisest among rulers in his day. He captures the modern idea that the more we know and the more we understand, the harder it is to pretend we don't know. Wisdom—the act of knowing what is right, fair, just, and orderly—will also bring grief as it brings peace.

Why, then, should anyone desire Wisdom's house if it brings grief or pain? Isn't that the domain of Folly's house?

It seems that from one hand wisdom restores a measure of peace to the soul, but the other hand brings the burden of seeing injustice more clearly. The hands combine so that the mind may connect foolish actions with inevitable destructive results.

The more we distance ourselves from our own folly and the hurt we have caused while indulging our own folly, the more our hearts likewise ache to watch the foolish destroy themselves, burn down their relationships, and betray the people around them. We hurt for them because we know the emptiness that awaits them at the end of their temporary pleasure. It's the same emptiness that we found at the end of ourselves that caused us to cry out for wisdom and life.

Solomon determines what is wise, possibly from his own experience with folly, his own folly and that of the people he ruled. Domestic issues, marital betrayals, crooked lawyers defrauding clients of their meager finances, thefts, murders, adulteries and other betrayals—too many grave injustices to name—were seen up close and personal by Solomon himself. Yet nothing is wasted in God's economy. As the king aged and as he pulled away from his own folly, God used his adjudicating of these situations to make him more wise.

His writing drips with the regret of a refugee who has visited the House of Folly more than once:

"Absolute futility," says the Teacher.
"Absolute futility. Everything is futile."
What does a person gain for all his efforts
that he labors at under the sun?
(Eccl. 1:2–3)

Better then to labor not under the sun, but under the Son. Christ is the source of all wisdom, and the only antidote to folly and destruction.

WISDOM'S HOUSE

"G et Wisdom, get understanding." Over at the House of Life, Wisdom is not looking for just a temporary visit from those she has called. She wants all who come through the door to take up permanent residence.

Once we set foot onto Wisdom's threshold, a whole new world lies before us. Like Dorothy opening the door from Kansas to Oz, the world we are about to enter will be drastically different from the one we knew as fools. We raise a hesitant fist; when she called aloud from the high points of the cities, did Wisdom really mean me? Her call was irresistible, but was it really for foolish little me?

Even before our fist raps the door, it opens. She has been waiting for us. Her hand reaches out to welcome us in like the father who ran to the prodigal, so glad is she to see us turn her way. The warm hand of help, truth, sincerity, and security takes us by the arm and guides us in.

Stepping through her door may feel like walking into a foreign land, stepping from the chaotic and clanging streets of folly to a wonderland of peace, justice, and order.

What is this place? So different from the one we tolerate across the street!

Is this the transition from the old man to the new? Is the threshold the margin between death and life?

At the same time, the new and unfamiliar world feels like coming Home: the capital *H* Home; Home to the conditions for which we were made.

Once inside, her door closes with a rich, velvet, and satisfying click of the latch. Security at last.

She offers us a tour. She introduces us to her maids, symbolizing worshipful service, cooperation, and simultaneous unity and diversity we see in the character of the Trinity. The way that the body of Christ should operate on earth, unified in mission and purpose, and in the object of their adoration.

Our brother Paul distinguishes what we should be from what we too often are:

> Now I urge you, brothers and sisters, in the name of our Lord Jesus Christ, that all of you agree in what you say, that there be no divisions among you, and that you be united with the same understanding and the same conviction. For it has been reported to me . . . that there is rivalry among you. What I am saying is this: One of you says, "I belong to Paul," or "I belong to Apollos," or "I belong to Cephas," or "I belong to Christ." Is Christ divided? Was Paul crucified for you?
> (1 Cor. 1:10–17)

We know that we are welcome, because this is where we were always supposed to be: near to the heart of Wisdom, close to the members of her household, and safely unified in Christ.

THE LEADER
LAYS IT DOWN

The LORD said to Moses and Aaron, "When Pharaoh tells you, 'Perform a miracle,' tell Aaron, 'Take your staff and throw it down before Pharaoh. It will become a serpent.'"

So Moses and Aaron went in to Pharaoh and did just as the LORD had commanded. Aaron threw down his staff before Pharaoh and his officials, and it became a serpent.

But then Pharaoh called the wise men and sorcerers—the magicians of Egypt, and they also did the same thing by their occult practices. Each one threw down his staff, and it became a serpent.

But Aaron's staff swallowed their staffs. However, Pharaoh's heart was hard, and he did not listen to them, as the LORD had said. (Ex. 7:8–13)

Have you ever heard seasoned saints share the Bible's wisdom? You can taste in their stories the God-given "life seasoning" as they toss details from memory into the pot and let them simmer with God's Word.

Sometimes the stories are bitter, sometimes tangy and spicy, sometimes pleasantly sweet. Life has its own way of flavoring what Scripture has already revealed to be true.

Years ago, I sat at the kitchen table of a wizened missionary. He and his precious and stalwart wife once smuggled Bibles behind the Iron Curtain during the cruelest days of the Soviet Union. He had certainly seen the good, bad, and ugly humanity of clergy and lay leaders in his day!

His eyes sparkled with faraway stories obviously playing on the screen behind his eyes, a screen that was out of view for everyone except him. Then those same eyes, full of memories, suddenly fixated on us at the table. He began to talk about the time when Moses and Aaron locked horns with Pharaoh's sorcerers in Exodus 7. He preached to us on God manifesting His glory and power in the faces of those who hated Yahweh and His people. He discussed the prophetic warning given that Pharaoh foolishly ignored.

And then . . . his eyes danced as he spoke of Aaron's staff.

"You see, when Aaron threw his staff down in Pharaoh's court as Yahweh had told him to do, he discovered the serpent that Yahweh said would be there." Yes and amen. If God says it, it is so, and you can believe it with all your heart!

Then the moment came when all the staffs in the court scene were thrown down, revealing serpents within. The snakes writhed and battled each other, until Aaron's staff devoured those of the sorcerers. What a terrifyingly tense scene that must have been.

Our brother leaned forward and lowered his voice to continue the story, nearly whispering:

"Now, up until that moment, Aaron had been helping to lead God's people, carrying the staff around, and completely unaware there was a serpent in it—until Yahweh told him." He went on. "Because Aaron's staff was given by Yahweh, the serpent He promised was under divine command to show His glory and power in Pharaoh's court. But because the magicians' staffs were in the service of idols and false gods, they were defeated and consumed by the display of glory of the One True God."

And when Aaron picked that staff back up, now likely several times heavier with the weight of the others ingested, what was object lesson was he left with?

Our brother concluded: "There's a snake inside every leadership staff, and that snake will do the bidding of whatever god we serve—false or true."

Wisdom's takeaway from Aaron's staff is this: We can be our own biggest obstacles to ministry and kingdom advance. Be careful with whatever measure of leadership God gives you. Whether it's at home, in our family, with friends, in ministry, the workplace, the world, whatever. Lay it down *constantly* for Yahweh's purposes and take it up with confidence . . . knowing whose house it serves.

THE WHO OF
MANIFOLD WISDOM

By reading this you are able to understand my insight into the mystery of Christ. This was not made known to people in other generations as it is now revealed to his holy apostles and prophets by the Spirit: The Gentiles are coheirs, members of the same body, and partners in the promise in Christ Jesus through the gospel. I was made a servant of this gospel by the gift of God's grace that was given to me by the working of his power.

This grace was given to me—the least of all the saints—to proclaim to the Gentiles the incalculable riches of Christ, and to shed light for all about the administration of the mystery hidden for ages in God who created all things. This is so that God's multifaceted wisdom may now be made known through the church to the rulers and authorities in the heavens. This is according to his eternal purpose accomplished in Christ Jesus our Lord.

EPHESIANS 3:4–11

God tells us through the apostle Paul that His wisdom is multifaceted. In some translations, the word is "manifold." This manifold wisdom is what makes plain that which seems mysterious, the hidden things of faith. The ways of viewing and understanding His wisdom is like looking at a prism.

Handle the prism itself, and we feel its many expertly made cuts covering its surface. Some areas are flat, wide, and smooth; some edges are beveled; others are pointed and even jagged, and still others have corners rounded by the craftsman's tools. Prisms are, in and of themselves, many-sided and intricately crafted.

Looking more closely, though, the prism's surface isn't the only aspect of its character. The cuts are designed to change sunlight into rainbow refraction, throwing about the internal elements that make up light itself. An exquisite crystal chandelier is made even more stunning when light passes through it, giving off living color dancing about the room, bouncing off skin and wall, beautiful to the eye yet impossible to ever capture with the human hand. Prisms come in many shapes—oblong, oblique, rectangular, irregular, hexagonal—yet they all refract the same rainbow light, in the same God-ordained order, reminding us of the same covenant-keeping God.

The mystery of God's handiwork is on display in the same way through His people. Having not only many features, colors, and languages, He tells us that, mysteriously, we will carry some of our earthly complexities to His throne through union with His Son. But the mystery deepens when we consider that this "set-apartness" exists not only around the globe today, but has always existed across historical eras, spanning time and space. God is keeping His own, and He refracts His covenant light through His people. He is harmonizing, calling, and keeping us in time and out, on earth and in heaven, until we assemble in His presence with our faith made sight, His spectrum of promise revealed in vivid technicolor.

We are created to display His manifold, multifaceted wisdom. Scripture tells us it will be an emotional time when God's people hear His voice in language never heard, yet still familiar, and we behold Wisdom Himself through refracting prisms of tears. What glory, when our Savior speaks over us:

Look, God's dwelling is with humanity, and he will live with them. They will be his peoples, and God himself will be with them and will be their God. He will wipe away every tear from their eyes. Death will be no more; grief, crying, and pain will be no more, because the previous things have passed away. (Rev. 21:3–4)

THE QUEEN

How far would you travel to grow wise?

The queen of Sheba heard about Solomon's fame connected with the name of the Lord and came to test him with difficult questions. She came to Jerusalem with a very large entourage, with camels bearing spices, gold in great abundance, and precious stones. She came to Solomon and spoke to him about everything that was on her mind.

So Solomon answered all her questions; nothing was too difficult for the king to explain to her. When the queen of Sheba observed all of Solomon's wisdom, the palace he had built, the food at his table, his servants' residence, his attendants' service and their attire, his cupbearers, *and the burnt offerings he offered at the Lord's temple, it took her breath away.*

She said to the king, "The report I heard in my own country about your words and about your wisdom is true. But I didn't believe the reports until I came and saw with my own eyes. Indeed, I was not even told half. Your wisdom and prosperity far exceed the report I heard. How happy are your men. How happy are these servants of yours, who always stand in your presence hearing your wisdom. *Blessed be the LORD your God!* He delighted in you and put you on the throne of Israel, because of the LORD's eternal love for Israel. He has made you king to carry out justice and righteousness." (1 Kings 10:1–9)

Some archeologists say the Queen of Sheba ruled modern-day Yemen. The first-century historian Josephus suggests she ruled a kingdom inside of Egypt or Ethiopia.

We simply know her as "the Queen" whose wealth, reputation, curiosity, and knowledge were an even match for Solomon. Whether she traveled from Ethiopia or Yemen, this honeyed, raven-colored figure brought her entire retinue of hundreds at least 1,400 miles to Solomon's land to test his wisdom—such was her hunger for this prized royal commodity.

And yet her journey to wisdom began with her first bejeweled step into her cortège. Royalty met royalty, power met power, and wisdom was exchanged. Perhaps Solomon told her that the source of all wisdom was available even to her, that all she need do was ask. That certainly would have been the wise thing to do, because she went seeking God's wisdom, not Solomon's. And Solomon knew it, and laid no claim on it for himself, but rather chose to give God the glory and let God's people enjoy the blessings.

Like Solomon, she desired neither prosperity nor power. The size of her company was more than proof of her success as a ruler; the four and a half tons of gold, the precious stones, and the largest quantity of spices Israel had ever seen satisfied the people's needs for a long time to come (1 Kings 10:10). She sought no geopolitical partnership, nor did she seek children like Hannah or Rachel. She didn't want to make a name for herself like Judas. She came not seeking power as an invader, but wisdom that could be gained from cultural exchange, perhaps even an interfaith dialogue.

She blesses him immensely for providing the key: wisdom comes not from Solomon, but from Wisdom Himself, the One she observes them worshiping, the one whose presence in their worship takes her breath away.

By seeking and desiring wisdom, this unnamed queen was already becoming wise; by acknowledging her lack, she found herself at Wisdom's door with her ebony hand poised to knock.

We, too, have a similar distance to cross. It's the spiritual distance between one house and another, the exchange of dwellings and affections, from living under the world's taskmaster to abiding in heaven's ruler. To make the spiritual journey is to travel from being far off to being near.

Despite the distances for the queen and for us, Wisdom's house is only a breath away . . . a prayer uttered, a breathless exclamation of wonder, or a life-giving, exhaled "yes" to follow Christ.

All new life in Christ begins with a breath—an utterance into the wisdom and hope of God.

Wisdom seekers constantly breathe this prayer, make the journey Home, and enter in.

19

SOLOMON'S
SHIFTING SAND

God gave Solomon wisdom, very great insight, and understanding
as vast as the sand on the seashore. Solomon's wisdom was greater
than the wisdom of all the people of the East, greater than all the
wisdom of Egypt. He was wiser than anyone . . .

1 KINGS 4:29–31

Earth's sands hold a few secrets of our wise Creator; from ocean
floor to hourglass, they too sing the mighty power of God.

A great part of the surface of the globe is covered by sand, the matter that shifts beneath our feet when crossing the beach or desert. We
think highly of sand when it does our bidding; it builds, it supports our
weight despite its shifting terrain, and we create colorful landscapes in
glass bottles that are, ironically, made of sand themselves.

We think poorly of sand however, whenever it becomes a nui-
sance: littering the bedroom floors from our beach excursions, pelting
our faces in the sciroccos of the arid desert plains, or becoming water-
logged, when quicksand sucks at our feet yet refuses to support our
weight. When sand is a collective, nature reminds us that we stand on
solid ground. Toss a handful on a windy day and see how weightless
and insignificant it is, as wind and gravity scatter its granules to new
resting places; such is the fickle nature of our feldspar-quartz cushion.

The sand on which we walk is pulverized by time, wind, water, and
pressure through the ages. It is steady and sure. When the particles are
bound together under the right conditions, they become immensely
strong. Sand is, indeed, a major commodity around the world, produc-
ing mortar, plaster, concrete, and asphalt paving. Mix it with clay, and

you have sturdier, even more tightly cemented bricks than those made of clay alone.

God promised Solomon that his wisdom would fill God's earth like sand, more numerous than the human hand can count. Yet with the promise came a warning, wherein the very nature of wisdom's sands also stands out. Only when Solomon's loyalty was turned toward Yahweh would his wisdom be a life-giving force; when he turned his knowledge and power on himself, he would become destructive:

> King Solomon loved many foreign women in addition to Pharaoh's daughter: Moabite, Ammonite, Edomite, Sidonian, and Hittite women from the nations about which the Lord had told the Israelites, "You must not intermarry with them, and they must not intermarry with you, because they will turn your heart away to follow their gods." To these women Solomon was deeply attached in love. He had seven hundred wives who were princesses and three hundred who were concubines, and they turned his heart away.
>
> When Solomon was old, his wives turned his heart away to follow other gods. He was not wholeheartedly devoted to the Lord his God, as his father David had been. Solomon followed Ashtoreth, the goddess of the Sidonians, and Milcom, the abhorrent idol of the Ammonites. Solomon did what was evil in the Lord's sight, and unlike his father David, he did not remain loyal to the Lord. (1 Kings 11:1–4)

Though Israel's king is remembered well for his wisdom, there were times when Solomon moved into Folly's house and knelt at the altar of self for earthly gain. Whenever he turned aside to forbidden women and their false gods, his wisdom dissipated and came to nothing but strife for him and his people—like so much shifting sand, scattered on the wind.

20

CONSEQUENCE, THE PROFESSOR

Blows that wound cleanse away evil;
strokes make clean the innermost parts.

PROVERBS 20:30 ESV

We learn some of our wisdom lessons the hard way; the burn teaches us that fire is hot, cruel and hateful gossip spoken aloud can't be taken back, spilled blood can't be reinserted into the lifeless body. The sluggard goes hungry, the adulterer is left high and dry by his secret mistress, the cheater is exposed to lose his ill-gotten earnings; deeds done in the dark are exposed to the light for disinfection and consequences.

Suffering teaches us to hate sin, and Wisdom sends Consequence to deliver our most severe rebukes.

It would be all too easy to believe these reveal God to be cruel and punitive, but such is not in keeping with the character of the God of the Bible, which tells us He is both perfect justice and perfect mercy. True to our human nature, when wrongs are committed against us, we cry for "justice," but when we are the wrongdoer, we cry out for mercy.

Our loving Father has given us a teacher to stand between Him and the pain, and that teacher is called the "natural consequences for our actions." Throughout Scripture, God brings blessings on His people for obedience, and curses for defying the moral and physical grain of His universe. Sir Isaac Newton captured this aspect of God's truth for all of humanity with his own pithy observation of God's physical world: "For every action, there is an equal and opposite reaction."

And so the consequences of our actions, whether those actions be true or false, stand as the greatest teacher. And when our actions are false or wicked, we suffer—and we learn. From the pain of a stubbed toe, to the justice meted out by local officials, to the burying of a body whose life we have taken—there are consequences to every action we make. This is a principle embedded in creation by Christ out of love, a desire to teach, discipline, and grow His own, a desire to maintain a just and civil world, and to display His glory for all to see.

And because He is both just *and* merciful, God doesn't leave us in despair at the hands of our consequences. Once repented of, He uses our sins to stand as teaching aids to ourselves and others.

Like an exquisite piece of Japanese pottery that's been dashed to the ground, He mercifully gathers the pieces of our sinful consequences, and joins them together with the precious gold of instructive redemption. As in *kintsugi*, the centuries-old Japanese art form poetically translated as "golden joinery," Christ rejoins our broken pieces using His own precious metals of mercy—gold, silver, platinum—so that the beautiful seams of gold glint in the visible cracks of our brokenness. The repair becomes an ornament, a testimony to God's faithfulness and His promise to redeem all things. The repairing of the breaches becomes a witness to His power, might, mercy, and glory, and as we grow wise, the smaller the cracks in our character become.

God's *kintsugi* process does not stop at a mere newly repaired vessel. No, while a new testimonial work of art is revealed in the "already" of life, He is also preparing the moment when all things are made new in His presence in our much anticipated "not yet" of glory.

In glory there is no need for repairs, there are no cracks, and there's no need for consequences. All things will be made holy and right in Christ, and in that place all will do right and be well forever.

21

THE LIBRARY OF WISDOM

Get wisdom, get understanding;
don't forget or turn away from the words from my mouth.
Don't abandon wisdom, and she will watch over you;
love her, and she will guard you.
Wisdom is supreme—so get wisdom.
And whatever else you get, get understanding.
Cherish her, and she will exalt you;
if you embrace her, she will honor you.
She will place a garland of favor on your head;
She will give you a crown of beauty. (Prov. 4:5–9)

The Al-Qarawiyyin Library in Fez, Morocco, is believed to be the oldest working library in the world.[1] It opened in AD 1359 at the University of Al-Qarawiyyin, which was established in AD 859. The library was the brainchild of Fatima El-Fihri, the daughter of a wealthy Tunisian merchant, clearly a lover of learning, education, and knowledge. Many other ancient libraries lay in ruins, victims of war and time. Yet archaeologists still painstakingly decode knowledge from broken shards of cuneiform tablets, so eager are we to know more about the world in which we live.

Meanwhile, the Library of Congress in Washington, DC, stands as one of the world's largest libraries, with over 173 million pieces catalogued. It's thrilling for bibliophiles—especially those who cherish print books—to know that there are people preserving culture, heritage,

---

1. Anna Todd, "You Can Visit the World's Oldest Library in Fez, Morocco," August 1, 2019, Discovery, https://www.discovery.com/exploration/Worlds-Oldest-Library-Fez-Morocco.

and knowledge of the ages so that we can wander in their stacks, turn to one side or the other, select a tome from the shelves, and sink into a forgotten era and turn the pages of long ago. To learn how people lived and loved, find the ways in which things work, explore the universe and man's inventions, and read of wars lost and won. To breathe deeply of the aroma of time, paper, history, and age is the fragrance of knowledge and learning.

The archivists, library scientists, archaeologists, and historians are the silent keepers of the written sum of man's wisdom, and its breadth and depth can't be understated. That's a lot of knowledge and, whether around the corner or around the world, we still turn to these hallowed places seeking knowledge that leads to wisdom. Access to such vast areas of man's knowledge and wisdom are made even more precious by knowing that interspersed among these dusty tomes, there are many who were actually thinking God's thoughts about the world He's created; this is the *only* way to think clearly about the world in which we live. In other words, women and men throughout history have sought to understand God's wisdom first, in order to inform their own, and their work has an eternal impact greater than those who started with their own limited understanding.

Despite our best human efforts, the wisdom of God needs an entire universe to express, reflect, and define itself to us; we only know Christ's world by Christ first teaching us. God drops more knowledge and wisdom into a simple wheat field than the sharpest archivist could ever drop while tripping up the library stairs.

Everything we need to know is in the person of Christ, in Wisdom Himself, since by Wisdom—Christ Himself—the foundation of the earth has been laid. We would do well to spend all we have to acquire Christ's wisdom, the wisdom that guards, the wisdom that guides, the wisdom that grants us favor and unshakable beauty.

For such knowledge and wisdom, there is only one cost involved: our know-it-all pride, for the doorway to Wisdom's house swings open by humility.

22

STAGNANT WATERS

On the last and most important day of the festival, Jesus stood up and cried out, "If anyone is thirsty, let him come to me and drink. The one who believes in me, as the Scripture has said, will have streams of living water flow from deep within him."

He said this about the Spirit. Those who believed in Jesus were going to receive the Spirit, for the Spirit had not yet been given because Jesus had not yet been glorified. (John 7:37–39)

Wisdom and life were made to be poured out onto others, not kept to ourselves.

When we abide safely in Wisdom's house and drink deep from her wellsprings, then by the power of the Holy Spirit streams of living water will flow from wisdom's life source into our hearts, and then onto others.

If a river loses its outlet, its water cannot stay clean. God has made it so that a steady water cycle provides life and provides it constantly. This principle is embedded in His universe.

Rivers find their source at their headwaters, perhaps from a sea, ocean, a bubbling underground spring, or melting snow. From their source, fresh water flows downstream creating river flow, gathering water and vapor from above and below. It carves channels of life throughout the landscape, bringing sustenance and gathering animals and communities to settle along its banks. It is the wellspring of daily human life as well; clothes are washed clean, dinners are made, children are born and grow older, spreading into the countryside in the quest for other streams; life continues. All the while, the current carries the flow along naturally, as if in a life of its own.

The river will flow until it finds sweet release at the end of its journey and the beginning of another, pouring from the river's mouth into a welcoming tributary, and start the self-cleansing, life-giving process all over again. The pool will evaporate, become rain, pour down, and restart its cycle as the river's source.

Until it doesn't.

If there is no flowing current—or worse, no outlet—the water gathers and quickly becomes a fouled cesspool, full of disease. With no current or outlet, still waters putrefy and emit vapors that destroy and kill. All of its immediate inhabitants suffer slowly, agonizingly. They don't even have to drink; proximity is enough to set the parasites swarming around any life that approaches. It begins to look like Folly's house, with toxic bacteria and deadly viruses breeding disease and death. Those that love decay and capitalize on death—flies, mosquitoes, larvae—congregate, looking for unwitting hosts to devour.

All our actions derive from a source, and their results prove in which house we dwell. They will reveal whether we've drunk from Wisdom's invigorating stream or have imbibed the sour contents of Folly's stagnant pool of death.

Once we are full of life, the river of life needs a mouth to speak life and all the riches it has found in Wisdom's home, so that it may release its overflow and cause more life to come. That's the nature of regenerative, life-giving wisdom; out of the overflow of the heart, the mouth speaks. Wisdom will flow into any heart that is willing to capture, receive, and start new life.

So from our mouths we speak wisdom, lest we become stagnant waters ourselves; we cannot keep the goodness of God's wisdom to ourselves. We speak Christ . . . and as we do, the Spirit flows from one to another, and so flows Life.

23

EVENING TO MORNING

God saw that the light was good, and God
separated the light from the darkness.
God called the light "day," and the darkness he called "night."
There was an evening, and there was a morning: one day.

GENESIS 1:4–5

In many cultures like my own, people clock their lives beginning with the morning hours and things concerned with awakening. Our eyes open after a night of rest to the insistence of our alarm clocks: sometimes music or chimes, and sometimes a rooster crowing outside our window if we're rustic enough. We begin the rituals that mark the day's passing, and as the sun sets, we wind down into the next night of rest.

Day descends into night, or so our bodies believe.

But this is not the order in which the writer of Genesis chose to mention the progress of a day; not dawn to twilight, but rather twilight to dawn. In the Bible's telling of the creation account, things are different: the dark comes first, then the light. In God's creation rhythm, night becomes day.

The writer of the creation account has one thing in view: marking our minds with the knowledge of God's sovereignty not only over the natural world, but the pattern of our souls. Even time is perfectly calibrated by wisdom for all we need. It's repeated with each day . . . *erev, boker, erev, boker*—evening, morning—repeated over and again, so that Wisdom establishes at creation a spiritual rhythm meant for understanding, our hope, and our growth as to how God sovereignly governs.

On the evening of His betrayal and sacrifice, Christ faced the manifold and collective weights of our lives—our sin, our fears, anxieties, worries, frustrations—the total effects of this fallen world. His own looming pain and suffering drove Him to pray in the darkness for our souls, gathering strength from His knowledge that dawn would come by His light, and by Him all shadows would disappear. He lays in the darkness of the tomb, and then comes resurrection morning for us all. Blessed dawn!

Zechariah prophesies of this thrilling moment of a new day when he beheld the Creator of the universe as an infant:

> Because of our God's merciful compassion,
> the dawn from on high will visit us
> to shine on those who live in darkness and the shadow of death,
> to guide our feet into the way of peace. (Luke 1:78–79)

And so it is for us. Without an end to the darkness of sin and hell and the grave we will not see the dawning of the new day in the new perfected city of God, our brilliant new Jerusalem. This movement from night to day is embedded in our salvation, in the cross, and in our basking in Christ's glory.

Blessed assurance, that darkness is defeated, that wisdom has placed light as both the finale *and* the beginning, and that the troubles of the night won't last always.

Even in darkness, we have the light of wisdom to mark the way.

There is wisdom and hope in the evening times, so we take heart . . . whether in the smallest heart pain or the greatest sin of humanity, the new day is coming. And indeed, has already come.

24

TARNISHED STAR

There has always been deep enmity between the houses of Wisdom and Folly. They have often stood face to face in one confrontation or another at historical and biblical intersections, with faithfulness meeting obstinance, hatred colliding with love.

This shouldn't surprise, since life and death stand in opposition to each other. Folly's resentment at being cast down goes deep.

> Shining morning star, how you have fallen from the heavens!
> You destroyer of nations, you have been cut down to the ground.
> You said to yourself, "I will ascend to the heavens; I will set up my
> throne above the stars of God.
> I will sit on the mount of the gods' assembly, in the remotest parts
> of the North.
> I will ascend above the highest clouds; I will make myself like the
> Most High."
> But you will be brought down to Sheol into the deepest regions of
> the Pit.
> Those who see you will stare at you; they will look closely at you:
> "Is this the man who caused the earth to tremble, who shook the
> kingdoms,
> who turned the world into a wilderness, who destroyed its cities
> and would not release the prisoners to return home?"
> (Isa. 14:12–17)

Enmity drove the serpent to upend our world with a tempting choice between life and death, faith and doubt, obedience and disobedience. The first man and woman threw away their inheritance and tilted the world by choosing violence and destruction. The crafty one met them at the place where their obedience was weak, and they forfeited their earthly and eternal real estate, as well as their perfect communion with

Wisdom Himself. The result is that we now live in their shattered shalom.

Their children fared no better. From the moment Cain's jealous rage at his brother's better sacrifice flowed through his veins to his fists clenched high—and when the death blow landed on Abel's flesh— Folly's enmity was on full display.

Death, opposed to life, seems bitterly resentful of those who leave and find abundant life and wisdom. Folly hates the indictment that freedom and new life bring down upon its head.

Whether it's God's prophets and sages confronting the people's self-destruction and wandering hearts, or whether it's Christ Himself driving the idolatrous money changers from His own house, those lovers of filthy lucre exploiting His people for their own gain and vainglory, the enmity is there. It is there as He confronts kings and rulers, and it is there when He confronts His own priests of temple renown. Wisdom shames Folly simply by its existence, striking awe in the hearts of the discerning. And therefore, whenever a Folly-dweller finds opportunity to harm a child of Wisdom, the age-old battle is engaged once again.

The promised showdown between the idol of man and the one true God, between truth and lie, between faithless religion and faithful worship, creates a cosmic cataclysm called the cross. Its resurrection power rearranged man's spiritual DNA and paid for our sins with such finality that we can once again stand before a holy God. It was an event so great that it obliterated every possible tomb for every man, woman, and child throughout history and set them free to escape every prideful, idolatrous tomb we insist on building for ourselves.

No wonder Folly and the agents of destruction are in a rage—the work of their master is completely undone. Folly's anger reaches its zenith at the end of days, when those who loved destruction and idols too much are divided from those who loved Christ more.

Even as Wisdom's guests join in the call to the foolish through inside and outside of the city gates, Folly-dwellers gnash their teeth, cover their ears, and persecute the faithful. Their hatred smolders in the ashes of their apathy and rebellion. Foolish Cains still grind their teeth, raise their fists, and beat and maim and kill.

And all the while Wisdom presses in with love, bids His own among them still . . . to come.

25

WISDOM'S
ULTIMATE VOW

Guard your steps when you go to the house of God. Better to approach in obedience than to offer the sacrifice as fools do, for they ignorantly do wrong. Do not be hasty to speak, and do not be impulsive to make a speech before God. God is in heaven and you are on earth, so let your words be few. Just as dreams accompany much labor, so also a fool's voice comes with many words.

When you make a vow to God, don't delay fulfilling it, because he does not delight in fools. Fulfill what you vow. Better that you do not vow than that you vow and not fulfill it. Do not let your mouth bring guilt on you, and do not say in the presence of the messenger that it was a mistake. Why should God be angry with your words and destroy the work of your hands? For many dreams bring futility; so do many words. Therefore, fear God. (Eccl. 5:1–7)

Let your words be few. The 1970s comedian Flip Wilson unknowingly quipped Solomon's wisdom in modern day language: "Never write a check that your body can't cash."

Though the preacher of Ecclesiastes declares that everything in life is meaningless time and again, God is anything but.

We needn't make extravagant vows or bargain with God over our future plans. We have nothing to bring to a table where God Himself is seated! We are outclassed, outwitted, out-planned, and out of sorts at our limited knowledge compared to His. There is no world in which we can offer God something in exchange for anything we desire, since we come with needful, empty hands. Contrary to every popular movie on the subject, the God of the universe simply doesn't do bargains.

So he who never makes a vow is better off than he who cannot keep the vows he makes, since the ultimate vow has already been made, and kept, when Christ gave Himself on the cross. His body wrote the cosmic check for us, paid our cosmic debt, kept the vow He made from the foundation of the world—that He would keep a people set apart for Himself, keep them safe through the generations, and fulfill all promises because He knew we could not. Through Christ, all bets are off. We are free to worship in Spirit and truth—no need to "swear oaths," no need for futile attempts at keeping them, no guilt over forgetting they've been made.

It's done.

In our worship, when we realize we are standing in the very presence of Wisdom, the wisest man advises that we say little and listen much—no vows necessary or even possible from our side of the cross. So we train our tongues to be still just as we would train our hands for battle; it's a discipline to learn to listen more than we speak.

> A wise old owl sat on an oak
> The more he saw, the less he spoke;
> The less he spoke the more he heard.
> Now, wasn't he a wise old bird?

26

WHEN CREATING
HANDS REDEEM

"I have fervently desired to eat this Passover with you before I
suffer. For I tell you, I will not eat it again until it is fulfilled in the
kingdom of God."

Then he took a cup, and after giving thanks, he said, "Take this
and share it among yourselves. For I tell you, from now on I will
not drink of the fruit of the vine until the kingdom of God comes."

And he took bread, gave thanks, broke it, gave it to them, and
said, "This is my body, which is given for you. Do this in remembrance of me." (Luke 22:15–19)

A generous host anticipates not only what each guest will need,
and not only what can be offered from the storehouses, cellars, and
pantry, but the host also knows in advance what his guest already loves.

When Christ says He fervently desires to eat this Passover with His
own, this word *fervently* is packed with the knowledge of the ages, the
preparations of the day, and the anticipation of the Lamb's Supper that
is to come in the glorified kingdom.

Our Lord had already scouted the location and sent ahead disciples
Peter and John to secure. They were to look for a man carrying a water jar,
a man who would stand apart from the crowd for doing what was cultur-
ally considered woman's work, which would mark him as doing the work
of the Lord. The room boasted enough space to hold a table that would fit
everyone chosen, everyone called, everyone appointed to be there, even
the betrayer who dwelt in Folly's house of destruction and self-will.

Who slaughtered the lamb at the appropriate sixth hour? Did John
and Peter perform the task? A priest, perhaps? Or did Christ slaughter
the lamb Himself?

As He thought of the lamb heading to slaughter, did Christ reminisce on the painful yet willing worship of Abraham, when he was asked to sacrifice Isaac and a ram was provided in the boy's stead?

Perhaps the imprint of the recent slaughter played through the preparer's mind as the horrific events unfolded. Tendons and bone, bloodshed, the last foreshadowed sacrifice before Christ's own for the highest purpose possible. Such thoughts might cause One to shudder before the words of resolve: "Lord, let this cup pass from Me; nevertheless, not My will but Yours be done."

Whoever the preparation fell to, everything was in readiness when the Twelve arrived, likely in small groups to avoid detection. The meal unfolded in the perfect hands of the One who had witnessed all the events necessitating sacrifice for our sin in the first place. The same hands that fashioned humanity and made man in His image now broke the unleavened bread and poured the wine, only now they worked to redeem creation rather than fashion it. The same mouth that breathed life into man was now infusing the Passover with fulfilled meaning.

Shed blood, broken body, new covenant. The imperfect and temporary Passover was fulfilled, and the new and eternal Passover had come.

In Proverbs, the meal Wisdom prepares for the simple is but a small picture of what awaits the disciples in the life of Christ, and what awaits us all in glory. Just as in Wisdom's house, place and details matter. They are an outgrowth of Wisdom's character, and they appeal to God's chosen as we all long for a table where we fit, that has been prepared, where we are welcome, and are forever changed for having accepted the invitation.

Wisdom Himself has set our table, and He knows what we need, what He offers, what we want, and what we love. He has commanded that we remember it as often as we are able, to sit and behold endless rows of platters overflowing with peace, love, redemption, forgiveness, and life. His food is nourishing and satisfies the fervent hunger of the soul.

And our greatest gift at the banquet—our Keepsake—is the flesh and blood, glorified presence of the Lamb.

27

THE VALUE OF
OBEDIENCE

The LORD rewarded me according to my righteousness;
he repaid me according to the cleanness of my hands.
For I have kept the ways of the LORD and have not turned
from my God to wickedness.
Indeed, I let all his ordinances guide me and have not
disregarded his statutes.
I was blameless toward him and kept myself from my iniquity.
So the LORD repaid me according to my righteousness,
according to the cleanness of my hands in his sight. With the faithful
you prove yourself faithful, with the blameless you prove yourself
blameless, with the pure you prove yourself pure, but with the
crooked you prove yourself shrewd. (Ps. 18:20–26)

It's as if the psalmist closed his eyes, strummed his instrument, and
whispered to his Maker: "This is what I love about you."

And then he begins to list the attributes of God that are not re-
strained within the Godhead, but rather pour out with great effect on
the world He has created. It is as simple as the natural physics of the
world, of divine cause and effect.

Christ is not like man with his hidden contractual clauses, tiny legal
details at the bottom of the document, or legal language whose terms
no layman can decipher. No, Wisdom Himself lays out the terms clearly
for His people to understand.

From the time Adam and Eve drew first breath in God's presence,
Scripture is shot through with blessing for blessing, and curse for curse:
"Do this and live, do that and you will surely die." Have we been overcome
with a fear of being labeled as legalistic? Or have we been overcome by

a strange Pharisee-phobia that takes our interest away from obedience and disobedience to God and His character? Perhaps we should call out to God and ask Him to wake up any among us who sleep on God's character, and the long-established grain of creation that teaches that living in wisdom and truth—even when it costs—brings earthly and spiritual blessing to those who claim His name.

> For you rescue an oppressed people, but you humble those with haughty eyes.
>
> LORD, you light my lamp; my God illuminates my darkness.
>
> With you I can attack a barricade, and with my God I can leap over a wall.
>
> God—his way is perfect; the word of the LORD is pure. He is a shield to all who take refuge in him.
>
> For who is God besides the LORD? And who is a rock? Only our God. (Ps. 18:27–31)

What we miss when we ignore that obedience brings blessing is the truth that there is power in the blessing. Receiving His power to endure and battle back against darkness and injustice and disobedience is a part of the blessing. Once delivered from the inhabitants of Folly's land of violence, Wisdom's reward is the power to beat the darkness back to Folly's door. For Christ, the Rock of Ages in whom we dwell, promises us that by His Holy Spirit He will build His rock upon His people's testimony of His greatness, and not even the gates of hell will withstand the force.

28

PRECISION, PREPARATION, PROVISION

God—he clothes me with strength
and makes my way perfect.
He makes my feet like the feet of a deer
and sets me securely on the heights.
He trains my hands for war;
my arms can bend a bow of bronze.
You have given me the shield of your salvation;
your right hand upholds me,
and your humility exalts me.
You make a spacious place beneath me for my steps,
and my ankles do not give way. (Ps. 18:32–36)

Our God supplies all our needs for when we journey outside of Wisdom's house. Once we are commanded to journey back into the city, Wisdom does not send us out unprotected, unclothed, or empty-handed—we leave fortified for the journey out and back.

By His wisdom, God has prepared us for every situation we may face. How quickly and smoothly the psalmist moves from clothed humans, to hooved animals, to images of men and women fit for battle.

For the psalmist, precision, preparation, and trust are the imagery of Wisdom's provision.

First to our clothes: we are wrapped in Christ's righteousness and His might, His wisdom and truth. A distinct image just for clothes-wearing humankind.

Then, to the deer. We have seen the images of a roe or fallow deer, or even the alpine ibex, ascending near-vertical mountain ledges, embankments, and dams, their cloven hooves effortlessly grasping the smallest ledges. Up they go in search for minerals and salts, their tongues flicking against the rock, seemingly oblivious to the dizzying heights they've achieved, much less the danger of the canyon far below.

Trust, power, stamina, and precision guide the herd as they travel difficult terrain together.

And then, the militaristic language, also communal in nature. We are made not only to grasp the bronze bow, but also trained in its proper usage lest we cause collateral damage and undue harm.

God is the Keeper. Every good and perfect gift comes from Him; wisdom, freedom, strength, humility, might, even the very ability to remain faithful comes from the power of His Spirit.

Can you imagine having to beat your own heart? He keeps His living machines running until it is time for them to come Home, and even the timing of our Homegoing is at His discretion.

All comes from Him, all is directed by Him, all is subsumed under Him, and all is given by Him.

With our God, we can scale a wall.

29

DEATH IS
UNNATURAL

The holey little holes In my skin, Millions of little Secret graves,
Filled with dead Feelings That won't stay Dead.
The hairy little hairs On my head, Millions of little Secret trees
Filled with dead Birds, That won't stay Dead.
When I die, I won't stay Dead.[1] —Bob Kaufman

The words of an obscure American beat and surrealist poet Bob Kaufman would make a fitting epitaph for a child of God. In his poem "Dolorous Echo," Kaufman focuses in on one specific, tiny life cycle God has put on display throughout the universe: the constant regeneration of his heart, his emotions, his fears, his joys, all expressed through the constant life cycle of his own body. Kaufman decides:

We were made to live, not die.

The wisdom of life is constantly on display, right before our eyes; it is so very near, so very clear. Bards throughout the ages have spilled much ink reflecting on life, beauty, and eternity in panoramic terms; some are wonderfully gifted with that special ability to turn phrases that speak of what our souls see and hear. Too often for us to ignore, they inadvertently speak truth of Wisdom's house directly to the Folly-dwellers. It's no surprise that though Kaufman kept company with those who denied God's existence, literary critics still hear in his work a poetic pondering that longs for some sort of immortality, perhaps even eternality. Though an admitted Buddhist, he still yearned for immortality—and here God was, faithful to reveal it to him through his own

---

1. By Robert Kaufman, from *Solitudes Crowded with Lonliness,* copyright © 1965 by Bob Kaufman. Reprinted by permission of New Directions Publishing Corp.

skin—his own God-made body that he wore every day.

Wisdom-dwellers and Folly-dwellers alike know that there is a God who created us, that He loves true Life for which we were created, that He hates our separation from it, and that He is not pleased that our lives have been given over to sin and death. And so He is constantly speaking to us through Wisdom's creation language, declaring to us "I AM."

> For God's wrath is revealed from heaven against all godlessness and unrighteousness of people who by their unrighteousness suppress the truth, since what can be known about God is evident among them, because God has shown it to them. For his invisible attributes, that is, his eternal power and divine nature, have been clearly seen since the creation of the world, being understood through what he has made. As a result, people are without excuse. (Rom. 1:18–20)

With each new dusk and dawn, the knowledge that God is present and ever-presenting Himself is displayed. This world, in its fallen state, fits like an ill-fitting shoe whose pressure sores remind us that despite Wisdom's imprint, this is not the world for which we were made. And so God shouts, and whispers, and shows Himself in and out of time through our living landscapes.

Scripture tells us that Kaufman is right. Whether one dwells together with Wisdom in Christ and enters His promise of salvation, or if one is left in the decaying house of Folly, everyone will eventually die—and live again. But to which life will they enter? A life set apart from the Creator Christ, or the one that is eternally separated from Him? For each of us will die, and none of us will "stay dead."

Only those who have been made alive to answer Wisdom's call, and who have repented to believe in Jesus Christ, will live in the glorious world for which we were created. Those who have wholly given themselves over to Folly, to the cares of the world and the pleasures of the flesh, will live a very different sort of life for eternity.

This is your moment to answer definitively. In whose house will *you* live?

30

MIRROR IMAGE

As water reflects the face,
so the heart reflects the person.

PROVERBS 27:19

We are entranced by our own image, borderline obsessive either by the satisfaction or dissatisfaction it brings. Snap a group picture, and we judge whether it needs a retake based on how *we* look! Whether on a camera or in the mirror, we often miss seeing more deeply than just our physical image. We miss that God's image is stamped on us, His living, moving, flesh machines with souls that need no external electrical wall outlets but somehow, by grace, manage to breathe, live, love, hurt and be hurt, and make more after our own kind.

There are few clearer and more absolute visions of God's image than our reflection in the mirror, but how often do we stop to regard the most obvious and persistent evidence of God's imprint on humanity? Whether it's visually tracing our features in a pool of water, in a quick side-glance in a shop window, or as we stand square on facing the mirror every morning and evening, multitudes of opportunities every day reveal to us that we are God's handiwork, the only artistry that bears Wisdom's image.

And yet every day, we walk away from the reflection that reveals the inconsistencies between our image and our actions. We look into the most penetrating mirror of all—the Word of God. Oh, that revealer of hearts that penetrates to the marrow of our motivations! We close the reflective book, forgetting that we were made for the life that wisdom brings—not the foolish actions that bring destruction to ourselves and others.

But be doers of the word and not hearers only, deceiving your-selves. Because if anyone is a hearer of the word and not a doer, he is like someone looking at his own face in a mirror. For he looks at himself, goes away, and immediately forgets what kind of person he was. But the one who looks intently into the perfect law of free-dom and perseveres in it, and is not a forgetful hearer but a doer who works—this person will be blessed in what he does.
(James 1:22–25)

We behold ourselves in the gospel mirror as we truly are, yet walk away ignoring what wisdom has shown us; that we are fallen, and des-perately in need of Christ's total redemption. We exult in the bold, gra-dient shadings of a perfect peach-tinged sunset, yet we turn away from it and step right over the wounded, grey-faced man lying in the street who bears the very image of God. What we ignore of self extends to what we are willing to ignore about others. When we forget our faces, we willfully crush and abuse our neighbor with our arrogance, self-righ-teousness, harsh and cruel words, and unjust actions.

Wisdom encourages the believer to watch our lives and doctrine closely to be sure there is harmony between what we know about God, and how we obey Him; it's of vital importance that our ethics and our epistemology match. Moreover, Christ gives the wisdom and power of the Holy Spirit to make this visage consistent as we reflect His character to the Folly-dwellers, so that their cries of our hypocrisy are empty.

How bold of Wisdom, to constantly remind us of who we are with-out Christ, and who we are with Him; that's a truly sober estimate. We have been set free by the law of liberty. We move out of the bondage of the house of Folly and destruction and enter through the open door the House of Liberty; the House of Wisdom; the House of Life.

Come to the mirror of the soul that shows you not only as you are, but as all that you are supposed to be.

How good of Wisdom, to save us from ourselves!

31

GIMME GIRLS OF THE GRAVE

The leech has two daughters: "Give, Give!"
Three things are never satisfied;
four never say, "Enough!":
Sheol; a childless womb;
earth, which is never satisfied with water;
and fire, which never says, "Enough!" (Prov. 30:15–16)

Imagine wandering slowly through the upper rooms of Folly's world, down the seemingly endless and winding dark corridors, with staircases that simultaneously, frustratingly take you everywhere and nowhere. Mazes that double back on themselves, dooming you to repeat the same paths over and over again in search of something new at the end, only to find the same dusty décor . . . and the occasional inhabitant.

Rounding yet another corner of confusion, you see two friendly figures down the hallway approaching you. You make out the silhouettes of young and attractive women, advancing toward you with smiles and outstretched hands. Their welcoming hands quickly turn to reaching and grasping, demanding from you what you do not have to give.

These are the children of Folly's guests, the offspring of parental leeches named Discontent and Entitlement. At first they were not unattractive—distance is a friend to death and decay. Yet as they draw close with their pleading hands, their smiles are desperate grins stretched across their faces. They carry the stench of unquenchable greed. Like the grave whose mouth is always open for more dead, they want your life. The twin sisters demanding according to their names "Give" and "Give" only live to consume their raging fire of need and expectation, and we are their eternal fuel. If we take that outstretched hand, we follow them to the grave: "Sheol and Abaddon are never satisfied, and people's eyes are never satisfied" (Prov. 27:20).

Like Adam and Eve in Eden's garden, the "Give" sisters turn to man—to themselves—to find what only Christ can supply. With no children of their own, they seek the children of others, only not to nourish them, but to destroy. The twins stand as a two-headed succubus, perpetually enchanted and seduced by the three temptations of Folly: flesh-lust that whispers, "I want it," eye-lust that proclaims, "I love it," and the pride of life that screeches, "I deserve it!" Rather than stretch their hands to God for what only God can satisfy, the sisters look to themselves. Not finding satisfaction there, they reach out to us, only to grab on and pull us into Abaddon, into the depths of hell itself.

But why should we grasp their withered hands, as if we can satisfy each other's abyss? We are not God any more than they! If we dare try to satisfy, we will be destroyed in the process.

Should you encounter these twins, battle against them with the truth, just as Christ did in the wilderness. Trust in faith that you have all you need in His hand of life. For it is written:

> Do not love the world or the things in the world. If anyone loves the world, the love of the Father is not in him. For everything in the world—the lust of the flesh, the lust of the eyes, and the pride in one's possessions—is not from the Father, but is from the world. And the world with its lust is passing away, but the one who does the will of God remains forever. (1 John 2:15–17)

32

A "SAFE SPACE"

When they say, "Peace and security," then sudden destruction
will come upon them, like labor pains on a pregnant woman, and
they will not escape. But you, brothers and sisters, are not
in the dark, for this day to surprise you like a thief. For you are
all children of light and children of the day. We do not belong
to the night or the darkness.
So then, let us not sleep, like the rest, but let us stay awake
and be self-controlled. (1 Thess. 5:3–6)

A re you looking for a "safe space"? Throughout human history,
humanity has searched for places to belong; a place where not
only their deepest needs are being felt, but also met. The longing in our
age for a place of safety, a place of shalom and security, is not new by
any means. Our generation has simply given a trendy new name to an
age-old longing.

But Scripture tells us that such a safe space as the world defines it is
actually a pale imitation of the reality of our hearts: our yearning goes
far deeper than a mere "safe space."

Just like many who came before us, and those who will come after
us, everyone longs for such a place, even those who can't admit it. The
desire for peace and safety is so ingrained because this was the orientation for which we were seated, and once upon a time the garden where
God placed us, satisfied us . . .

. . . but man.

The pull for such a place is so strong, that we attempt to manufac-
ture it, even temporarily, for ourselves and those we love.

Historians in eras to come will certainly look at our seemingly "modern" longing for safe spaces, and what this says about the uncertainty of

the environment around us in this peculiar age. But how can one possibly feel completely safe in a world that—because of us—holds a default setting to folly, disappointment, injustice, evil, and pain?

It's no wonder we feel insecure. Our concept of a safe space is dictated by what makes us comfortable, which may or may not hold for everyone. Yahweh as a safe space is defined by what agrees with God, which always and ultimately works out for everyone's good.

From the days of Adam and Eve, who shattered their own shalom and found themselves alienated far from the One who loves and cares for them most, He has still remained more than a safe space. He has stood the test of time as their strong tower, a house built on wisdom's foundation, in and through His Word.

He saves His own into Wisdom's house through His own abiding obedience to the Father's will and assures us that we may also walk the path in His footsteps. We can find perfect shelter and safety only in Him, both in this life and the next.

> My son, don't forget my teaching,
> but let your heart keep my commands;
> for they will bring you
> many days, a full life, and well-being.
> Never let loyalty and faithfulness leave you.
> Tie them around your neck;
> write them on the tablet of your heart.
> Then you will find favor and high regard
> with God and people.
> (Prov. 3:1–4)

33

RIGHTEOUS OAKS
DON'T MOVE

The Spirit of the Lord GOD is on me, because the LORD has anointed me to bring good news to the poor.

He has sent me to heal the brokenhearted, to proclaim liberty to the captives and freedom to the prisoners; to proclaim the year of the LORD's favor, and the day of our God's vengeance; to comfort all who mourn, to provide for those who mourn in Zion; to give them a crown of beauty instead of ashes, festive oil instead of mourning, and splendid clothes instead of despair.

And they will be called righteous trees, planted by the LORD to glorify him. (Isa. 61:1–3)

Scripture doesn't embody wisdom in a pastor, a therapist, a trained counselor, a theologian, or the pithy words of a cultural influencer. Proverbs doesn't embody wisdom as your favorite teacher, author, activist, or artist.

No.

Proverbs shows wisdom in an everyday person who grows up into a mighty oak of righteousness—tall, formidable, and majestic, weathering the harshest elements that weather can throw its way. The conditions only make its roots stronger and deeper, its bark tougher, its boughs wider and host to new life. This is a person who knows life's pains intimately, and who knows God even more intimately than that pain. Wisdom is a deep believer who does her best to love the people around her by living wise and timely application of God's intentions in their ordinary, everyday life.

Wisdom exists to make the simple strong, where in our fallen humanity we unnecessarily complicate navigating life. Wisdom is gracious in making herself available to everyone, and it's through acquiring wisdom that good shepherds, life-giving therapists, healthy counselors, accurate and ethical theologians, cultural influencers, authors, activists, and artists may grow.

God's wisdom remains the only wisdom that delivers us from the prideful and toxic folly of self-destruction, and the only soil in which a wise forest of believing trees may grow. Below the soil's surface, the taproot drills deep into the ground to maintain its constant supply of Living Water, sending shoots out in a thousand different directions that anchor it from wind and wave.

Meanwhile on the surface, the trees by the water lean out over the banks of their bayous with fierce determination to remain planted firm, despite their boughs' gravity-defying feats. The trunk stays strong, from one generation to the next.

Our roots matter. The Source from which our roots drink matters. The fruit we bear—it all matters. Walk with the wise and become wise. Walk with the foolish, and we are a party to our own destruction.

> How happy is the one who does not walk in the advice of the
> wicked
> or stand in the pathway with sinners or sit in the company of
> mockers!
> Instead, his delight is in the LORD's instruction, and he meditates
> on it day and night.
> He is like a tree planted beside flowing streams that bears its fruit
> in its season,
> and its leaf does not wither.
> Whatever he does prospers. (Ps. 1:1–3)

Thank God today for the wise and mighty oaks of righteousness He has placed on your horizons and choose where you will stand. In the words of the African American spiritual:

> I shall not, I shall not be moved;
> I shall not, I shall not be moved.
> Like a tree, planted by the water . . .
> I shall not be moved.[1]

---

1. Alfred H. and B. D. Ackley, "I Shall Not Be Moved" (1908). Found in *Pentecostal Hymns* (Chapel Hill, NC: University of North Carolina, 1911), 10, https://www.youtube.com/watch?v=02UAYQSNAvE.

34

CELEBRITY IS UNNATURAL

The more we study the creation account and Wisdom's commandments in the book of Genesis, the more that human celebrity appears unnatural.

Though we are the only creature to bear God's image on earth, we were not designed to bear the weight of idolization. God, in His wisdom, did not include it in His creation package, because we were created for the sole purpose of worshiping Him alone.

Humankind wasn't made to bear the scrutiny—nor the expectations—that idol makers demand. The load is too heavy for the human heart, mind, and body to bear.

So when we hear Wisdom's call to bring worship aright, in obedience, when we take our proper place and lift our eyes to the only one who is deserving of all praise, the invitation under our no-win conditions of our fallen world is a sweet one. Freeing. Even divine.

When we look at the true and living God as He has revealed Himself to us in Spirit and truth, we become persuaded at the futility of raising men and women to celebrity or even idolatrous status. It not only destroys us and dashes our hopes and expectations that they be what they cannot, it destroys them in the process.

Idolization is a drug for the idolater and for the object of worship alike. If not handled well, internal and external pressure creates fissures and cracks in the soul: idolatrous toeholds for both worshiper and the worshiped. Shall we drag people from the streets by the scruff of their necks into Folly's house with the lure of false worship? Shall we be complicit in their destruction and ours? The only way a person can bear being adored, praised, and recognized by multitudinous hordes without being destroyed is when such recognition comes as a grace of God for

His purposes. Then He provides the strength to bear it wisely and well.

Wisdom's command to "have no other gods before Me" doesn't merely protect our communion with God, it protects us from destroying ourselves, and from destroying others.

Idol worship is too heavy a burden for us to bear . . . worship is reserved for the Creator alone. Run fast and run hard into the arms of the only true and living God.

So, whoever thinks he stands must be careful not to fall. No temptation has come upon you except what is common to humanity. But God is faithful; he will not allow you to be tempted beyond what you are able, but with the temptation he will also provide the way out so that you may be able to bear it.

So then, my dear friends, flee from idolatry. (1 Cor. 10:12–14)

35

TINY IDOLS,
OUR IMAGE

Little children, guard yourselves from idols.

1 JOHN 5:21

We can imagine that Folly's house is full of tiny idols. Statues great and small litter her home, representing the things we love and cling to that hinder our complete worship of God.

If this were so, these idols would not only line the shelves on walls, they would be stacked in darkened corners, buried in root cellars and boxed above the head in attic rooms: the relics and totems that defined our affections and drove our basest instincts to protect them at all costs.

Anything that is absolutized without God becomes an idol, subject to collapse with a propensity to oppress others. In other words, when we only focus inward and gaze at ourselves, someone outside of us must be the ideal and someone must be less than that ideal.

As we search through the idols that litter Folly's house, it's inevitable that we will find one that looks just like us. The idols we set up tend to look an awful lot like us and, if we're generous, like our tribe who conforms to our likeness. If left unchecked by God's ever-searching Spirit, the secular lie of self-esteem can lead us to self-adoring, self-absorbed circles and become a cultural shackle that binds us. We use and discard the less than ideal and reduce them to mere utilitarian purposes, as pawns to serve the world I've created in which "my will be done" is the rallying cry—history tells these tales in every age and era.

How, in our present age, do we break these chains that drag us kicking and screaming back to Folly's Apollyon?

We break the chains the bind us when we esteem the One in whose image we are made. The shackles fall when we cease attempts to make others over in our image. We find freedom when we respect the intentional design of a transcendent Creator who has uniquely made His entire creation for His own kingdom purpose. This interrupts the destructive cycle of pain that our idols inflict and minimizes their influence over ourselves, our families, and our communities.

To paraphrase C. S. Lewis: Our idols will cease to be devils when they cease to be gods.[1]

---

1. See C. S. Lewis, *The Four Loves* (New York: HarperOne, 2017), 8.

36

IGNORANT, LOUD, DANGEROUS

Folly is a rowdy woman; she is gullible and knows nothing. She
   sits by the doorway of her house, on a seat at the highest point
   of the city,
calling to those who pass by, who go straight ahead on their paths:
"Whoever is inexperienced, enter here!"
To the one who lacks sense, she says, "Stolen water is sweet, and
   bread eaten secretly is tasty!"
But he doesn't know that the departed spirits are there, that her
   guests are in the depths of Sheol. (Prov. 9:13–18)

In the town where Folly and Wisdom reside, the image gives the impression that one can simply move between houses quite easily—buildings numbered 8 and 9, if you will, at the cul-de-sac on Proverbs Lane.

One may even be able to see one house from the window of the other. A Folly-dweller might be able to throw a rock or steal a pie cooling in a nearby window. A Wisdom-dweller might battle the weeds and vermin that creep from her careless neighbor's unkempt backyard. The idea of physical proximity is there in the image.

Yet when it comes to fruit in keeping with obedience, there is great distance and difference between their character and reputations. The spiritual gulf between them and the kind of people they produce, foolish or obedient, is vast.

Make no mistake. Folly is no lady and her house is no home. She is not even close to being a woman, but rather a cheap, pale imitation dressed garishly as what she considers Wisdom to be. Sometimes, when she puts in the effort, she can pass herself off as something close to Wisdom, but something out of sorts will always tell on her, make us turn our heads in doubt and suspicion. She is never what she appears to be, and neither are her promises.

When we answer her call, she will rob us not only of the courage of our convictions to do right and act justly but steal our very convictions themselves. The gullible and the rowdy become nearly parasitic on one another, as the easily swayed are lured by the fiery and false. Oh how they love trouble and dissension!

All of creation produces after its own kind, even the spiritual forces. Like her father, the author of destruction and the lord of lies, Folly attempts to imitate Wisdom with the exact same words spoken by truth: He who is inexperienced, enter here! But like the garden's serpent, there is the twist that adds the temptation: "To the one who lacks sense, stolen water is sweet and bread eaten in secret is tasty!" Like her father, the devil, Folly's promise is similar—but not the same—as the promises made by Wisdom, who is full of transparency and integrity, who has painstakingly baked her own bread and mixed her own wine. For Wisdom's call is solemn, transparent, and true:

"Whoever is inexperienced, enter here!"
To the one who lacks sense, she says, "Come, eat my bread,
and drink the wine I have mixed.
Leave inexperience behind, and you will live; pursue the way of understanding."
(Prov. 9:4–6)

The Creator's wisdom dictates that His universe's creatures create after their own kind. Folly is like her father, the father of lies, theft, and destruction. She leaves in her wake inbred generations after their own kind: false teachers with doctrines that prize earthly and selfish gain and make themselves into petty gods, dictators who destroy tens of thousands, and all those unfaithful to God who pose as abusive and deceptive "friends."

These are the descendants of Folly, the generations who follow that ancient pattern of enticement to savage the simple and create more of their own kind. They leave destruction and despair in their wake, even after they have long departed from this world.

37

MOVING DAY

The one who walks with the wise will become wise,
but a companion of fools will suffer harm.

PROVERBS 13:20

What must it have been like to walk with Wisdom and Creation Himself? We'd like to think that in the presence of living Wisdom, in the presence of Christ Himself, we would hang on to every word because every word was His Word and every word was Wisdom. I imagine even in Christ's most intimate discussions, beautiful pearls fell from His mouth each time His lips parted to speak. How much more were His actions, suitable and perfectly appropriate for every moment.

Jesus' disciples didn't fully grasp who they were speaking to. Some, like Peter, understood that He was *the* Christ, *the* Messiah, the long-awaited One and the fulfillment of prophecy. Not even Peter had the full picture in the pre-resurrection days, like most who knew of Jesus' fame. It's almost as if most in the region were expecting the Messiah to be either a prophet, a priest, or a king as in the days of old, but being all three was difficult to grasp. No, not all three—not necessarily eternal, not all-powerful, and certainly not crucified, dead, and buried. It took the illumination of the resurrected Christ and the Holy Spirit to guide them into the fullness and magnitude of His truth.

At what point did the disciples believe? At what point did they realize that Jesus fit the description?

In the beginning was the Word, and the Word was with God, and the Word was God. He was with God in the beginning. . . .
He was in the world, and the world was created through him, and yet the world did not recognize him. He came to his own, and his own people did not receive him. (John 1:1–2, 10–11)

Judas—that unbelieving devil (John 6:64, 70–71), that thief (John 12:6)—stands apart from the disciples in ignoring, even exploiting, the Wisdom alongside whom he walked. He built an external company of fools who were bent on Christ's destruction, as it only benefited their own selfish ambitions. He met Folly's promise head-on, in his own destruction. As for the other disciples, we can't quite pinpoint the precise moments when the faithful ones believed. Though many walked away, others answered Wisdom's call to emerge from the seas, from the trees, and even later on the road to Emmaus—they walked with Wisdom.

For many, traveling the dusty roads with Christ in His flesh was a one-step-forward, two-steps-back proposition; sometimes they responded with wisdom, other times they gave way to folly and fear. But when He proved His resurrection to them face to face, they believed and received power from on high to remain obedient to new life in Him. They walked with Wisdom anew for a time, saw Him with fresh eyes of understanding, had their minds illumined, and moved away from foolishness and darkened understanding toward true wisdom and light.

Jesus moved His disciples from Folly's house to Wisdom's home simply by walking alongside His own. And so it is with us, in the beautiful, companion-based process of life together that we call *discipleship*, so named after those who experienced it first. As we walk together, we see hearts renewed by the washing of the Word, reorienting foolish and destructive thoughts and habits in favor of ones of life-giving wisdom. Rancid thinking, along with the actions that cripple us and others, become fewer and further between, and more disciples join the eternal train.

Promising to never leave us nor forsake us, He still walks with us through others who are growing wise. The movement from foolishness to wisdom, doom destruction to purpose, from death to life, is our gift to one to another as we walk together with glorified Wisdom Himself.

38

FOLLOW ME

As he was walking along the Sea of Galilee, he saw two brothers, Simon (who is called Peter), and his brother Andrew. They were casting a net into the sea—for they were fishermen. "Follow me," he told them, "and I will make you fish for people." Immediately they left their nets and followed him.

Going on from there, he saw two other brothers, James the son of Zebedee, and his brother John. They were in a boat with Zebedee their father, preparing their nets, and he called them. Immediately they left the boat and their father and followed him. (Matt. 4:18–22)

Come this way . . . follow me. Wisdom personified in Proverbs 8 gives us a glimpse of how Christ would walk the earth when He came to us the first time . . . wandering the highways and byways, calling out to the simple, and bidding them "come."

Christ moves like Wisdom, says the things that Wisdom says, does the things that Wisdom does, because He Himself is pure Wisdom.

And so destructive Folly is the offspring of the crafty serpent; he has produced after his kind. Life-adorned Wisdom likewise emerges as creation, truth, and justice imbued with Christ's character. This is the pattern of the universe.

He walks all of His creation's terrains, calling from dusty roads carved out by chariot wheels and horses hooves, to cobbled stone roads, and side streets packed down with dirt of the ages; cultivated fields and untamed steppes, synagogue halls and corrupt courtrooms, private homes and upper rooms; once, seemingly impossibly on water, and finally—the hellish and humiliating trudge down the Road of Sorrows, to the cross at Calvary.

All the while, summoning and calling . . . *Come.*

From Bethlehem to the Jordan, from Nazareth and Capernaum, from Galilee to Bethesda, to the final shaking of Jerusalem itself seated on a humble donkey, everywhere true Wisdom walked He called and imbued His true followers afresh with His own purpose, passion, renewal, and redefinition:

To Folly's demons, He commands, "Depart." To His own, He beckons: "Come."

He calls through cupped hands to James and John: "I will make you fishers of men!"

He cries aloud to Zacchaeus, high up in the tree: "I will change your household from folly to wisdom, from deceit to truth!"

The call that caressed His own mother at the beginning of His earthly journey, calling her name through the angel Gabriel: "Bring Me into the world and be blessed!"

It is Christ's imperative "Come," the wise embodiment of His Person, Passion, and Presence that construct a new anatomy of a life exchanged, and that provide the core of every disciple's identity. A whole new person merges from the shell of the old, when He bids us "Come." Wisdom from fall, death to life, blind to sight, crippled to healed.

In a global atmosphere of confusion over the essence of personhood, the image of God upon us, and identity confusion, Wisdom's call creates the most thorough identity transition one can ever make.

And His call is still there for us to answer: "Follow Me, and live."

39

GROPING FOR
THE DOOR

The price of wisdom is beyond pearls. . . . Where then does wisdom come from, and where is understanding located? It is hidden from the eyes of every living thing and concealed from the birds of the sky. Abaddon and Death say, "We have heard news of it with our ears."

But God understands the way to wisdom, and he knows its location. For he looks to the ends of the earth and sees everything under the heavens. When God fixed the weight of the wind and distributed the water by measure, when he established a limit for the rain and a path for the lightning, he considered wisdom and evaluated it; he established it and examined it.

He said to mankind, "The fear of the Lord—that is wisdom. And to turn from evil is understanding." (Job 28:18b, 20–28)

Not every guest in Folly's house is decaying, lazy, or perverse; there are those inside who are wandering around, looking for the door to get out. The temporary circumstances of life that cause fear, doubt, and worry may have brought them to Folly's chambers, yet they can hear Wisdom's call filtering through the openings in slats and the cracks in the doors into their ears and hearts. Quickened, they are desperate to find their way from her darkened parlors, into the sunlight of Wisdom's new dawn.

This life is hard and profoundly disappointing, and there are times when grief and suffering overwhelm and lead us to seriously consider committing foolishness and destruction ourselves. Yet when we hear wisdom's distant call to come to our senses, an urgency returns to our search for the door, and we grope in the shadows for any door to trust and peace.

We may never fully understand why suffering and pain visit our own personal doorsteps, but we can avoid folly in times of trouble by treasuring God's eternal, redemptive purposes for all loss and pain.

The wisdom to know that sometimes we will not be allowed to know why sin and Satan has made this life so incredibly hard, when it's actually a special providence of God. It's in this place where Wisdom becomes a balm for our questioning souls; truth, justice, and faith were made for times of suffering, but those are all nonexistent commodities in Folly's house.

Consider the Lord's servant Job.

Job lost almost more than one person can bear. Reputation, health, wealth, and security, property, the people who served him and relied on him for their security, his own beloved children and, at times, his mind; even his friends. Surely the one profound question that rang through his God-recognized righteousness was "Why?"

But though Job's fears, pains, and doubts led his well-meaning friends to Folly's front door, they found no solace for him there. In the place where Folly makes destruction and death, Wisdom is only a rumor, unseen and not believed: "Whatever your hands find to do, do with all your strength, because there is no work, planning, knowledge, or wisdom in Sheol" (Eccl. 9:10).

With the ugliness of pain exposed, Job waxes heavy on the cost and value of wisdom in a cold and barren winter season of life.

And so Job offers us this exquisite poem on his meditations on wisdom. He sings not only of the precious value of wisdom—greater than pearls, rubies, and gold—but also of its elusive nature. God, in His mercy, has hidden some of His plans from us that would otherwise be too great to bear, saving them up to reveal when the sands flow from His hourglass to fill our empty soul-vessels of faith. What is revealed of His purpose behind our suffering is enough, and what is His secret is kept, in love, by Him for His own perfect timing. We cannot figure it all out, the cause and effect of one tragic event to yield life in another; He who knows and sees all things plans and executes it for us.

Our only role is to let Him lead us away from further folly and find our way back to Wisdom's house again where the healing balm of time may be applied.

40

THE TAIPEI 101

"Therefore, everyone who hears these words of mine and acts on them will be like a wise man who built his house on the rock. The rain fell, the rivers rose, and the winds blew and pounded that house. Yet it didn't collapse, because its foundation was on the rock. But everyone who hears these words of mine and doesn't act on them will be like a foolish man who built his house on the sand. The rain fell, the rivers rose, the winds blew and pounded that house, and it collapsed. It collapsed with a great crash."

MATTHEW 7:24–27

One foggy New Year's Day, young Kaitlyn lay in the hospital after a horrific car crash. Just three months before, the twenty-four-year-old college graduate had led her church in a song that proclaimed Christ as her firm foundation.[1] The song's sweet, rocking lullaby in six-eight time worked against the profound, earth-shattering jostling of life and circumstances for all the hearers, as if a central force who intimately knew all the forces of the universe undergirded the song and moved the worshipers in time to the musical lilt.

The imagery she sang was powerful, of an unmovable Rock on which she had planted her feet, and though the earth gave way around her, the place where she kept her feet stayed was solid ground—all because of her faith in Jesus, who had never let His own fall in the shifting chaos of life. Her sweet soprano voice declared that her God would never fail, singing "He won't, He won't" . . . not knowing that she would need that resolve just a few weeks later as she lay in the hospital fighting for her life.

---

1. "Firm Foundation (He Won't)," Maverick City Music, feat. Chandler Moore and Cody Carnes, Capitol Christian Music Group, 2021.

As her family gathered in prayer vigil around her, they recalled her singing just weeks before. They played the recording for family and friends and encouraged them to stand on the Rock, though the earth was shifting and seizing around them all. As the band played in the quiet interlude on the recording, Kaitlyn's own voice told of her childhood obsession with tall buildings and architecture. She spoke of one of the tallest buildings in the world she'd learned of as a child, the Taipei 101, and how it was built on earthquake-prone terrain. The architects had placed a dampening sphere high atop the building in its core. When an earthquake or high winds buffet the building's great height, the damper controls the sway and keeps the building so stable that the inhabitants won't feel nature's effects.

Yet the counterbalance high atop the Taipei 101 would not work without a sure foundation below. The taller the building, the longer the steel must be in the ground to steady it.

Some engineers and architects committed to the wisdom of sound structural and moral integrity take an oath pledging excellence to think such things through and keep us safe. They wear a stainless-steel ring on their little finger that keeps them in constant contact with the structure they're building. In the same way, our great Architect keeps His own constant contact—His steadying hand—upon the structural and moral integrity that upholds our lives. Though Satan should buffet and trials should come, the blessed assurance controls that all will be well in His hands.

A few days later, with the comforting prayers and voices of friends and family, and even her own voice in song drifting in and out of her consciousness, the Christ of Kaitlyn's song became her reality. After many days in care, Jesus carefully encircled her soul in an eternal hug, and carried her to the great heights of Wisdom's home, that eternal place where nothing crashes, quakes, wounds, or harms.

The Architect's arms became her perfect sphere and sure foundation. Those fortified arms did not fail, and she made it safely through.

And so will we all.

We are assured that Christ handles every homebound saint with this same tender care and assurance, so very precious in His sight is their death, and also the new life of His much-loved saints.

41

CANCER, RUST, AND GANGRENE

"Wisdom is better than strength, but the wisdom of the
poor man is despised, and his words are not heeded."
The calm words of the wise are heeded more than
the shouts of a ruler over fools.
Wisdom is better than weapons of war, but one sinner
can destroy much good.

ECCLESIASTES 9:16-18

Cancer. Rust. Gangrene. Each one difficult to cure, each one hard to detect until the damage shows itself. They all spread in stealth, and quietly advanced their undermining destruction long before we realize that they are even present.

Though Folly's call is loud, her effect also spreads quietly like corrosion, seeping into the cracks of what is good, right, and true. She never misses an opportunity to exploit a weakness.

Her corrosion is a slow burn covered by a thin veneer of godly paint—but soon enough her rust and stain bubbles through and proves that she has eaten away at once-decent metal, weakening whole structures if we do not take care.

Despite Wisdom's warnings about Folly's destructive intentions, the passersby still choose Folly. Why do we always fall for Folly's seductions when history so consistently shows the fate of the fool?

She does her work in every era, every epoch—even among those who name Christ's name. Not even the religious leaders who handle the Word of God are immune. It is especially serious when Folly infiltrates leaders who are tasked with guarding Wisdom's gates. When they are duped, their people are exposed to stealthy, rapidly spreading exploitation that should have stayed outside of Wisdom's fence.

Wisdom calls the simple, but she does not call the scornful, for though they hear they will not heed.

> You were running well. Who prevented you from being persuaded regarding the truth? This persuasion does not come from the one who calls you. A little leaven leavens the whole batch of dough. I myself am persuaded in the Lord you will not accept any other view. But whoever it is that is confusing you will pay the penalty. (Gal. 5:7–10)

Wisdom is better, but not heeded; Wisdom is greater, but not heard; Wisdom is tasted, but not trusted. And so Folly spreads and does the work of a cancer, hindering the good that Wisdom has accomplished. More than once, the apostle Paul warns us about Folly's false teachers, how their gangrene spreads and corrupts good in the body's healthy flesh:

> Be diligent to present yourself to God as one approved, a worker who doesn't need to be ashamed, correctly teaching the word of truth. Avoid irreverent and empty speech, since those who engage in it will produce even more godlessness, and their teaching will spread like gangrene. (2 Tim. 2:15–17)

Christian leader, take heart. Stand firm in Wisdom. Neither Folly, nor her father Satan, nor any of her stiff-necked guests will have the final word. They cannot stop what God has begun from the foundation of the world. Wisdom will have her final say. Bless the Lord today, for He has established His throne in heaven. Our weapons are not the weapons of the world. Wisdom, truth proclaimed with the timing of God, stills stand in our arsenal—wield her. He cuts out the rot with wisdom and mercy when we speak His truth. He will build His church on the rock of true wisdom, and against it the gates of hell and destruction will not prevail.

Growing wise will be a frustrating proposition . . . grow and exercise wisdom anyway, in spite of this fact.

42

SHARPEN THAT AX, SON

If the ax is dull, and one does not sharpen its edge,
then one must exert more strength;
however, the advantage of wisdom is that it brings success.

ECCLESIASTES 10:10

A young country preacher took his text on a humid Sunday morning, pleased to have been invited as a guest to speak. The church pianist had just retired the congregation to their seats after the hymn, and as tambourines were laid to the side and fans waved away the heat, the upturned faces of a spiritually well-fed congregation smiled a collective expression of holy expectancy.

The time had come for the Word.

A row of humble, suited elders dressed in their Sunday best lined the front pew. This old guard punctuated the young preacher's sermon with shouts, hand waves, and the repeated, encouraging "Amen."

As the message progressed, it took more than a few subtle turns away from the text, in favor of the preacher's presumptions stated as scriptural fact. As the flock heard more opinion than Scripture, more thoughts of men than of God with conclusions that were actually offensive to the God of life, the amens died down and a hush fell over the congregation. Pages that had once rustled excitedly stopped turning, and only the handheld fans continued to wave.

The young man, sensing the shift in mood, closed his Bible and brought his sermon to a close. Having finished, he slumped in his guest seat among the elders.

The elder seated next to him kindly patted him on the arm and whispered, "It's all right, son. I think your ax was sharp, but your handle was weak."

Ecclesiastes tells us that the work is easier and the results better when the ax head is sharp and precise. This is true whether it's wood chopping or surgery—a dull edge makes everyone involved suffer . . . the craftsman, project, and patient alike. The old elder that Sunday picked up on this truth, and more: not only must our ax heads be sharp and precise, but our handles must be strong as well to rightly divide the Word, to know the truth, and to refuse its compromise; for even around the Word of God, the battle between Wisdom and Folly is joined:

Continue in what you have learned and firmly believed. You know those who taught you, and you know that from infancy you have known the sacred Scriptures, which are able to give you wisdom for salvation through faith in Christ Jesus. All Scripture is inspired by God and is profitable for teaching, for rebuking, for correcting, for training in righteousness, so that the man of God may be complete, equipped for every good work. (2 Tim. 3:13–17)

Study to show yourself approved. Therein lies the carpenter's apprenticeship, the skills of applying God's wisdom in the right way and at the right time, both in what we say and in what we do. To do that which pleases God and thwarts the devil and Folly's schemes.

In truth, do we know our Bibles well? Some may know and misapply pieces because we've not been taught that there is one story that coheres from Genesis to Revelation, and that its proper telling and living pleases the author and finisher of our faith. Of course, in times where we are unintentionally imprecise, God's wisdom is sure and His aim true. That the Word will still do the work it has set out to do—and that, dear students of the Word, is the Holy Spirit advantage—guaranteed to increase our skill as we learn, and promised success that His Word will not return void, even in our weakness.

There is no better time than today to begin sharpening blades and strengthening handles, to learn to wield well the wisdom that's been placed in our hands. It's the only weapon that cauterizes the wound as it slices through heart and souls of men.

43

GETTING IN
FOLLY'S FACE

> I have observed that this also is wisdom under the sun, and it is sig-
> nificant to me: There was a small city with few men in it. A great king
> came against it, surrounded it, and built large siege works against it.
> Now a poor wise man was found in the city, and he delivered the city
> by his wisdom. Yet no one remembered that poor man. And I said,
> "Wisdom is better than strength, but the wisdom of the poor man is
> despised, and his words are not heeded."
>
> **ECCLESIASTES 9:13–16**

In Greek legends, Cassandra, the beautiful daughter of King Priam, was gifted by the mythical god Apollo with the gift of seeing and foretelling the future. After she spurned Apollo's advances, however, he punished and doomed her divination by ensuring she would never be believed. The futility of it all drove her mad, making her even less believable with every word she spoke.

Thank God this is not so with the proclamation of God's wisdom, even though many will remain unmoved when Wisdom speaks. There is often little recognition for speaking God's wisdom. God's cautionary wisdom is dismissed not because it is untrue or illogical, but largely because it is unwelcome, costly to both flesh and pride. Yet the prophets looked beyond the futility to the hope of Yahweh, and the promised rewards for obedience gave the prophets and their hearers the hope needed to stand on Wisdom's promises.

The preacher's words here conjure visions of Israel's real-life wilderness prophets, those ages of sages who shot arrows of wisdom and sacrifice straight into companies of folly and rebellion, their warnings often falling on deaf ears.

Ecclesiastes' preacher draws a picture of the lone prophet in a city, wisdom pouring from his lips yet remaining ignored. This unknown poor man's futility conjures a cascade of historical images: the solitary prophetic figure fleeing the city for his life only to grope the walls of a dark cave and stumble upon seven thousand who had chosen obedience and loyalty over destruction and folly (1 Kings 19). Another lay for more than a year on his left and right sides for the sins of God's people (Ezek. 4:4–8), and still another walked naked (or nearly so; some scholars believe he would have been wearing a loincloth) and barefoot for three years (Isa. 30:2–4). They all called to God's people and their neighbors to turn away from foolishness and face the living God.

Listen and live!
Repent for the kingdom of God is near!
Come and eat, all you who are simple!

Speaking wisdom in the face of folly will be a thankless proposition . . . speak and do wisely anyway, in spite of this fact.

FOLLY NEVER FULFILLS HER PROMISES

> A wise person's heart goes to the right,
> but a fool's heart to the left.
> Even when the fool walks along the road, his heart lacks sense,
> and he shows everyone he is a fool.
>
> ECCLESIASTES 10:2–3

Wisdom and Folly do not often travel together. Though they travel on divergent roads, their reputations still stand in opposition to each other and create stark contrasts all over their small town. Shadow and light, death and life, the two embed themselves in the natural world and their differences are on display for the whole town to compare.

In the natural world, the heavier a bomb's destruction, the more likely we will notice the tree stubbornly breaking through a broken wall. Notes of hope rise from a lone cellist seated amid rubble, caressing his city with a solo against the smoldering rebar of his town square. The more desperate Folly makes the room, the brighter Wisdom shines to say, "Take comfort, I am better and I am here."

And often, Folly will tell on herself, if given enough time.

False religions and their gods always prove themselves bankrupt. Since they work on the law of diminishing returns, their inevitable failure provides the backdrop for the hope of the gospel. Since Folly has no way of redemption or healing, the promised utopian society never materializes but descends into hatred and chaos, and promised equality means everyone gets nothing—not even life itself.

Folly's very character betrays her plans. She has no discretion, no discernment, no hope; she is pointed in who she targets, but reckless in her attacks; her way is sloppy. Folly's exposure is the time for Wisdom's people, the body of Christ to shine with their hope in the life, death, resurrection, and glorification of Christ.

By adventure, I do not mean "seven days and six fun-filled nights of wonder and excitement." Rather, I mean adventure in the sense that we will be taken into the desolation that Folly has caused, to places where our faith and confidence are stretched, proven, and deepened, where meaning is given to the pains, disappointments, and sufferings of life. As we affirm our commitment to all the things that Christ is—wisdom, life, hope, and sacrifice—He becomes that tree breaking through the rubble; we become the cellist's song of hope and deliverance in the town's square. We live as the set-apart people we have been redeemed to be.

And that is the contrast.

Signs of life in the midst of devastation are set there for our benefit, for our hope in ongoing darkness, whether these are the effects of war, the trauma of abuse, or the persistence of depression.

Wisdom gives, then, as a gift. Our task as we wait for the exodus from Folly's house? To help each other as we become mired—often through no fault of our own—and suffering in Folly's darkness.

45

DOWNRIGHT MEAN

If the ruler's anger rises against you, don't leave your post,
for calmness puts great offenses to rest.

ECCLESIASTES 10:4

There are times when Folly turns mean and violent. She wants to yell, scream, blame, and brawl.

Yet I would hazard that most people who have unwittingly encountered her spirit don't know how to fight.

Not even fight well, but fight, period.

Most of us don't want to. Many of us don't know what we would do if a fight broke out around us, although I would think most hope we would do the right thing, whatever that may be.

We might fight back. We might freeze. We might flee. It's likely that most of us hope that we'll never have to find out. Yet more and more the citizens of our world indulge Folly's nature, filling the earth with brawlers and murderers. Folly's vitriol fills our screens with rage against her fragility, vomiting violence over offenses real and imagined.

And wisdom tells us to keep calm? Lord, help.

Our bodies tell us that one thing is essential to keeping one's head when, as Rudyard Kipling once wrote, "all about you are losing [their heads] and blaming it on you,"[1] hurling doubt, invective, swearing, pointing, and even lying and scandalizing your name face to face, noses so close as to almost touch.

The one thing we must do to stay calm in the face of assault is breathe.

Calm breathing regulates our racing heart rate from a gallop to a

---

1. Rudyard Kipling (1865–1936), "If," written circa 1895.

standstill. It sends sweet oxygen to our panic-stricken brains. Our life's breath is our eye in Folly's hurricane.

The breath of life is a powerful thing. All of life begins and ends with our breath. God breathed His life's breath into only one creature, humankind, and animated us as flesh-covered, living souls. At birth, the newborn fills her lungs for the first time, and issues forth that declaration cry: "I live!" And when our eyes close on this world at the end of this life, our last breath ushers the believer into our Savior's presence, and, if we are secure in Him, into life as it was always supposed to be.

> Breathe on me, Breath of God,
> Fill me with life anew,
> That I may love the way you love,
> And do what you would do.
> —Edwin Hatch[2]

And so we breathe, out and in, out and in. Suddenly we are calmer than the one accusing, seeing things with eyes of life and not death, seeing more humanity than folly before us. Wisdom has mercifully pulled us back into her house for further instruction, before we move ahead.

Wisdom says do not be controlled by another who is under the sway of Folly's anger and malevolent bile. The Creator's breath slows the pace of a heart rate set to racing by confrontation.

A reasonable person may well back down. An unreasonable one may not, and more choices will have to be made.

But before all else . . .

Breathe.

---

2. Edwin Hatch (1835–1889), "Breathe on Me, Breath of God," https://hymnary.org/text/breathe_on_me_breath_of_god.

46

WISDOM'S AGONIES,
OUR CRIMES

And he came out and went, as was his custom, to the Mount of Olives, and the disciples followed him. And when he came to the place, he said to them, "Pray that you may not enter into temptation."

And he withdrew from them about a stone's throw, and knelt down and prayed, saying, "Father, if you are willing, remove this cup from me. Nevertheless, not my will, but yours, be done." And there appeared to him an angel from heaven, strengthening him. And being in agony he prayed more earnestly; and his sweat became like great drops of blood falling down to the ground.

And when he rose from prayer, he came to the disciples and found them sleeping for sorrow, and he said to them, "Why are you sleeping? Rise and pray that you may not enter into temptation." (Luke 22:39–46 ESV)

If Christ is the One who established wisdom's rule . . . if He is the One who is sovereign over all the affairs . . . of all the people on earth . . . if He is in absolute control of it all . . .

Why is He in such agony on this fateful night?

He is in agony because He voluntarily took on flesh and experienced the worst of the worst in this life. We are but dust; none among us can raise our clay fists at Him and cry, "You don't know what it's like to be me!"

No one can accuse Him and say, "You don't understand the darkness I feel."

No one can ever look at Jesus and cry out, "You don't know my pain, my sorrow, my sadness, my confusion, my loneliness, my fear, my . . ."

He knows.

He took on flesh and walked the joys *and* the sorrows of our lives. He knows. He knows all the insults and pains that will be thrown at those who will bear His name.

Even just on this night alone, look at the indignities He suffered: every indignity that the house of Folly could hurl at Him; a plot hatched by the religious establishment in cahoots with the state to murder Him; a hit on an innocent man. The plot extended into the courts, carried out by a deceiver on the inside—Judas Iscariot—one of His own.

In front of His own betrayer, with full knowledge of the extent of the evil in their hearts, He submits to the plot. They dip their hands in the bowl, and Jesus could have grabbed him by the wrist and given him the what-for right then, but no. He encourages Judas to "go do that which you must do and do it quickly." When an assassination attempt is discovered against earthly leaders, everything is done to stop the perpetrators, but not so with the King of kings. He lets the plot play out and is betrayed to the authorities with an unholy kiss.

He watches the folly of His disciples squabbling over possession of His legacy.

He knows already the cut of Peter's denial the next morning that he was ever associated with Christ whose name has, by now, become a scandal in the region.

And later, as the wicked chaotic night unfolds and plods toward the cross, He endures a mockery of a trial, the twisting of His words, the beating of His flesh, public humiliation of carrying His own cross through the streets, and then hanging naked and exposed from that cross for crimes He didn't commit.

Our crimes.

The indignities of the story match the agony of the prayer.

And when facing the agony of the ultimate indignity of the intersection of Wisdom and Folly, Wisdom Himself prays, and bids us to pray.

Knowing the indignities Folly has brought to this world . . . He prays.

And so then must we.

47

FOLLY'S BETRAYAL

The Festival of Unleavened Bread, which is called Passover, was approaching. The chief priests and the scribes were looking for a way to put him to death, because they were afraid of the people. Then Satan entered Judas, called Iscariot, who was numbered among the Twelve. He went away and discussed with the chief priests and temple police how he could hand him over to them. They were glad and agreed to give him silver. So he accepted the offer and started looking for a good opportunity to betray him to them when the crowd was not present. (Luke 22:1–6)

The upper room scene is crowded yet intimate, peopled yet private. Every gesture at the table is pregnant with fulfillment and meaning, from the pouring of the wine to the sharing of the cup, to the breaking of the bread, and then . . . the charge to "do this in remembrance of me" (Luke 22:19).

Everything old about this feast of unleavened bread is now new.

All that the disciples anticipated about the coming of Messiah is literally being fulfilled, in real time, by the hands of Jesus Himself.

And also in this moment, destruction lurks beneath the surface of it all.

Just as Satan intruded and shattered the peace of the first man and woman in the garden, Satan also audaciously enters this scene too . . . reclining at the table, Satan has taken up residence in the heart of one very willing Judas Iscariot.

"Truly I tell you, one of you will betray me."

The disciples started looking at one another—uncertain which one he was speaking about. One of his disciples, the one Jesus loved, was reclining close beside Jesus. Simon Peter motioned to him to find out who it was he was talking about. So he leaned back against Jesus and asked him, "Lord, who is it?"

Jesus replied, "He's the one I give the piece of bread to after I have dipped it." When he had dipped the bread, he gave it to Judas, Simon Iscariot's son. After Judas ate the piece of bread, Satan entered him. So Jesus told him, "What you're doing, do quickly."

None of those reclining at the table knew why he said this to him. Since Judas kept the money-bag, some thought that Jesus was telling him, "Buy what we need for the festival," or that he should give something to the poor. After receiving the piece of bread, he immediately left. And it was night. (John 13:21–30)

There, at that table, Folly and Wisdom meet. The two dip their bread in the same bowl and betrayer meets betrayed. Cain versus Abel. Death versus Life. Establishment versus Movement. Deception versus Truth. Violence versus Peace. Self versus God. Violence meets peace, arrogance meets humility.

The Judas faces the Christ, and Folly and Wisdom are now intimate, face to face.

Perhaps fingers even brush together in the bowl of betrayal as Folly is exposed for all of history to see.

How many of the indignities we also suffer are relational? Reputational? Even personal? All human beings know that the wounds from those we love and trust can be some of the deepest.

"That which you must do, do it quickly," Jesus says. And the pregnant, prophetic moment fades to black as Judas leaves the room.

At the center of each of these highly dramatic scenes is Christ, heaven's man, heaven's rule.

Wisdom and knowledge have been at the center of everything from the beginning of time, planning justice imbued with mercy, making the wrong things right.

48

WHEN WISDOM
PRAYED

Then an angel from heaven appeared to him, strengthening him.
Being in anguish, he prayed more fervently, and his sweat became
like drops of blood falling to the ground. When he got up from
prayer and came to the disciples, he found them sleeping, exhausted from their grief. "Why are you sleeping?" he asked them.
"Get up and pray, so that you won't fall into temptation."
(Luke 22:43–46)

Our Lord's first line of defense against anxiety is to pray. Doctor
Luke, who records these events and knows wisdom's hand on the
human body, brings us to three important points about anxiety in our
flesh:

In His flesh, Jesus anticipated His first and once-in-a-lifetime separation from the Father, which would cause Him to cry in anguish from the
cross, "*Why?* Why have You forsaken me?" Yet Jesus knows the darkness
of this separation so well that, after His resurrection, He promises us He
will never leave nor forsake *us*. Once we are united, He will *never* leave nor
forsake His own, especially in our darkest hour. He knows—from a flesh
standpoint—that it is terrifying to be alone.

Jesus would, for the first time, know the anguish of sinful rebellion
and human regret, carrying forgiveness for each person's lifetime of sin
for time immemorial, every sin of our past, our present, and even our
future. Claiming sin and the effects of every cruel and careless word,
every beating, every lie, every rape, every torture, every murder, every
genocide, every cruelty, and every offense against humanity that man-
and womankind could devise, so that *we* wouldn't have to bear it.

He also knew He faced a long, slow, and literally excruciating death.

Ex crucis—meaning literally "from the cross." This pain was *excruciating* of a particular kind, drawn from the prolonged death-drain-by-cross that shattered the bodies of not only of its victim, but the psyche of all who witnessed their agonizing suffocation.

The intersection of these agonies is medically real: "hemosiderosis" is a product of severe mental distress where the capillaries expand from stress and our sweat literally becomes bloody. For our precious Lord, this was the weight of the pain of the cross and our sin that infused every pore and cell of His body.

And yet—and this is stunning—despite the anguish and anxiety and the anticipation, the One who rules heaven, the One who set the world in motion from the beginning of time, who set the stars in the sky, who calmed the seas and can still the waters, who knows how His body will be wracked by pain within twenty-four hours . . . He. Still. Prays. for the events that Wisdom Himself has set in motion from the foundation of the world; "nevertheless, not my will, but yours, be done" (Luke 22:42).

And what does His prayer yield? He receives strength from on high in His flesh and weakness to endure the brutal, burdensome task that is to come. Angels come and minister to Him and He's supernaturally strengthened—*not to escape the agony, but He is empowered to pray more fervently to endure it.*

Wisdom's prayer produces even more fervent prayer. The more one prays, the more one is moved to pray.

In praying, Christ moved in His humanity from anxiety to adventure. And I don't mean "adventure" such as a vacation, or a hike, or a treasure hunt, or into an unknown land full of pleasure and delight. No.

Rather, He walks where no man could walk: to the cross on our behalf, from humanity to the cross then to Sheol to lead the captives out of captivity, to sit at the right hand of the Father to wait and intercede and claim, for His own, that which we could never claim for ourselves.

He walked the road from destruction to life, from folly to wisdom, so that we could take up our cross, follow Him, and live.

49

OUR WISEST PRAYER

As the disciples walked along the path following Wisdom Himself, they made a crucial and honest request:

"Lord, teach us to pray!"

As He obliged, He shared what is most important to Him, and He makes a distinction between how the wise and the foolish pray:

"And when you pray, you must not be like the hypocrites. For they love to stand and pray in the synagogues and at the street corners, that they may be seen by others. Truly, I say to you, they have received their reward. But when you pray, go into your room and shut the door and pray to your Father who is in secret. And your Father who sees in secret will reward you.

"And when you pray, do not heap up empty phrases as the Gentiles do, for they think that they will be heard for their many words. Do not be like them, for your Father knows what you need before you ask him. Pray then like this:

'Our Father in heaven,
hallowed be your name.
Your kingdom come,
your will be done,
on earth as it is in heaven.'" (Matt. 6:5–10 ESV)

The essence of the prayers that rise from Wisdom's house come from true Wisdom's lips: "Not My will, but Yours be done." We all know this prayer so well, many of us from memory. How often do we gloss over these words: "Your will be done"?

In them we hear the same words Christ prays on the night He was betrayed, in the tense air of Gethsemane. He prays as He taught, even commanded, us to pray.

When we pray in His words, "not my will, but Yours," we pray for at least three things:

First, we pray to accept God's will.
Second, we ask to approve God's will.
Third, we pray to do God's will on earth as in heaven.

Christ has not asked us to do anything that He Himself has not already done, or to pray as He has not already prayed. "Not my will, but Yours" is a prayer after Wisdom Himself that is sure to make life, to make peace, to stir up kingdom trouble, to discern heaven and earth.

This is a prayer to make one wise.

50

WISDOM UNIFIES

I have given them the glory you have given me, so that they
may be one as we are one. I am in them and you are in me, so that
they may be made completely one, that the world may know you
have sent me and have loved them as you have loved me.

JOHN 17:22–23

Wisdom unifies. For the body of Christ, "one" is more than a
number; it's a state of being. Christ's people are one, because
Christ's wisdom has determined in prayer that they should be so.

On the eve of Christ's greatest trial, we find Him on His knees,
sweating in a garden alone, offering His heavenly Father a three-fold
prayer: for Himself, for His disciples, and for future generations of believers who will bear His name.

This prayer for our unity offers three striking clues to the significance of the "oneness" Christ achieved through this wise, life-giving,
unifying prayer.

He's already cautioned the disciples that the world would hate
them, just as it has hated Him. Folly-dwellers will roll their eyes, gnash
their teeth, bite and devour in hostility over the unity that was set in
motion in that first garden long ago.

Our oneness with Him is connected to our unity with each other.
There are no other earthly relationships that are based on physical and
spiritual union with the entire person of Christ. And this oneness together is so precious, so unique, that it makes us in Him a different
people altogether, different from any other people group or culture
or ethnicity on earth. The houses of Wisdom and Folly could not be
more different.

Though our earthly relationships and concerns may have earthly significance, they are not Christ's primary focus at this hour. Christ's prayer for unity and endurance is formed, uttered, and accomplished with only one relationship on His mind: His relationship with us, and our relationship with one another.

He prays over us to His Father: "Make them one as we are one." In an instant, we are reminded that our relationship with Him is intimate, Christ-centered, physical, and distinct.

There simply is no comparison to any other earthly alliances.

To be one with Him, and one with each other . . . this is the Father's will, this is Christ's will, and the work of wisdom from the beginning of time, united with those who were always His from the start.

This is the sweet place where Wisdom gathers His own.

Just as the prayer of submission to the Father's will led Christ to face the cross and physical death, the prayer is also the strength we need to face the tasks we have been given. We are to make disciples of all nations, baptizing them in the name of the Father and the Son and the Holy Spirit, to make His name great to all nations, and to show the broken world what justice and shalom are like under Wisdom's rule.

51

OUR FINEST
HOUR?

Wisdom has prepared the church to live her finest hour, no matter what age she is in.

"Dear friends," Peter wrote, "don't be surprised when the fiery ordeal comes among you to test you, as if something unusual were happening to you. Instead, rejoice as you share in the sufferings of Christ, so that you may also rejoice with great joy when his glory is revealed" (1 Peter 4:12–13).

He continues: "If you are ridiculed for the name of Christ, you are blessed, because the Spirit of glory and of God rests on you. Let none of you suffer as a murderer, a thief, an evildoer, or a meddler. But if anyone suffers as a Christian, let him not be ashamed but let him glorify God in having that name" (vv. 14–16).

We should expect to suffer the same indignities as Christ, because we are one in Him.

But we should also expect that He will strengthen us by the wisdom that undergirds the universe to endure all the way to the end.

Peter closes out this passage, reminding us:

For the time has come for judgment to begin with God's household, and if it begins with us, what will the outcome be for those who disobey the gospel of God?

And if a righteous person is saved with difficulty, what will become of the ungodly and the sinner?

So then, let those who suffer according to God's will entrust themselves to a faithful Creator while doing what is good.
(1 Peter 4:17–19)

How in the world do we possibly abide in Wisdom's house when Folly's call is so strong and her hatred so deep?

How can we rejoice as we share His sufferings?

How in the world do we combat the shame Folly heaps on Wisdom as we resist her dark forces against humanity and against God's people?

Evil *will* press in. It is promised, and it is inevitable.

Strength begins with praying Wisdom's prayer:

Yet not my will, but Yours, Lord.

This is our strength in suffering that reminds us in whose house God's children dwell. It is still the house of hope, even when it is hard:

> The Spirit himself bears witness with our spirit that we are children of God, and if children, then heirs—heirs of God and fellow heirs with Christ, provided we suffer with him in order that we may also be glorified with him.
>
> For I consider that the sufferings of this present time are not worth comparing with the glory that is to be revealed to us. For the creation waits with eager longing for the revealing of the sons of God. (Rom. 8:16–19 ESV)

Wisdom has promised us troubles, the same troubles He Himself has known. Yet it's by Wisdom's forward-looking hope that we overcome.

52

REST AWHILE

"While I was with them, I was protecting them by your name that you have given me. I guarded them and not one of them is lost, except the son of destruction, so that the Scripture may be fulfilled. Now I am coming to you, and I speak these things in the world so that they may have my joy completed in them.

"I have given them your word. The world hated them because they are not of the world, just as I am not of the world. I am not praying that you take them out of the world but that you protect them from the evil one. They are not of the world, just as I am not of the world. Sanctify them by the truth; your word is truth.

"As you sent me into the world, I also have sent them into the world. I sanctify myself for them, so that they also may be sanctified by the truth." (John 17:12–19)

Here is the world," Frederick Buechner says. "Beautiful and terrible things will happen. Don't be afraid."[1]

The world outside of Wisdom's door can seem terrifying. Monsters and temptations lurk behind beautiful seascapes, wolves in sheep's clothing peek out from nature scenes, shadows and specters make us hesitate to venture outside. But there are people out there as well . . . people waiting to hear wisdom's call from our lips.

And so we set our eyes on Him, and not on the shadows that lurk. We step gingerly, cautiously, and yet boldly into the world of those caught between life and death. We know their fears, concerns, and idols because they once were our own.

We breathe an intrepid sigh and ask Wisdom to make Himself known amid the most difficult circumstances.

---

1. Frederick Buechner, *Wishful Thinking: A Theological ABC* (New York: Harper & Row, 1973), 34.

The answer that comes is enlivening. Christ grants the wisdom and knowledge of not only what to do, but the strength to do it. He tenderly loved the eager, the indifferent, and even His persecutors into His kingdom, and away from the ways of the world. He gives His people the power to stay single-minded on His mission, and not yield to Folly's hypnotic siren call.

Yes, we will see Folly-dwellers do horrific things. We may witness evils large and small. But Wisdom gives boldness to seek justice in the "nasty now-and-now," but also to trust the assurance of perfect justice in the "sweet by-and-by."

Wisdom gives the courage and strength to, even at the last breath, love the salvation of even those who hate.

Wisdom walking among the land of Folly marks us not merely as countercultural, or apolitical, or even antipolitical, but as "other cultural" and "other political" altogether—a whole other culture, with a set of politics based on the life, death, resurrection, glorification, and heavenly rule—of Jesus Christ.

Oh, to be more and more like Him in our dark and troubled times, just as He became like us in His!

He knew what it was like to be us.

He still knows what is to be us.

He's given us the way to be like Him.

The Man of Sorrows and the Wisdom of Heaven. Two faces commingled in the same person, and wholly given to us for our comfort and courage.

Does Folly's world frighten you? Is your mind exhausted by destruction and hate? Are you weary to the bone?

The world is a wearying place. Rest with Wisdom for a while.

Trust.

Pray.

And then go.

53

ELOQUENT
SILENCE

Just as Wisdom grants us persevering faith and disruptive speech, He also grants us eloquent silence. This is the space between the notes of music, the pause in the action of the story, the hush falling over the crowd. Eloquent silence can hold more truth than words could ever say.

> They led Jesus away to the high priest, and all the chief priests, the elders, and the scribes assembled. Peter followed him at a distance, right into the high priest's courtyard. He was sitting with the servants, warming himself by the fire.
>
> The chief priests and the whole Sanhedrin were looking for testimony against Jesus to put him to death, but they could not find any. For many were giving false testimony against him, and the testimonies did not agree. Some stood up and gave false testimony against him, stating, "We heard him say, 'I will destroy this temple made with human hands, and in three days I will build another not made by hands.'" Yet their testimony did not agree even on this.
>
> Then the high priest stood up before them all and questioned Jesus, "Don't you have an answer to what these men are testifying against you?"
>
> But he kept silent and did not answer. (Mark 14:53–61a)

The religious leaders gathered in special session that night to interrogate the One who would fulfill everything they knew about Yahweh. He stood in front of worldly esteem. And they couldn't see who He was.

Their calumny was rank, as was their arrogance. The irony of their arrogance . . . the students positioning themselves to review the Teacher on the accuracy of His views.

The kangaroo court of chief priests and religious leaders paints the picture of students against Master, false witnesses against Truth, false religions against true worship, disobedience against obedience, idol against God, ignorance against all knowledge, and of course, Folly versus Wisdom.

Believing themselves wise in their own eyes, the proceedings' agenda was to cross-examine and expose a false prophet. Yet blinded by rage at the weakness of their own idols by comparison, they failed to see that prophetic fulfillment stood before them in the flesh.

And so Jesus held His peace. He will not answer to lies, because He is truth, and He makes no defense because the prophecy must be fulfilled.

And the priests missed even this prophecy fulfilled, before their eyes.

"He was oppressed and afflicted, yet he did not open his mouth. Like a lamb led to the slaughter and like a sheep silent before her shearers, he did not open his mouth" (Isa. 53:7).

And in His likeness, there are times when we too will be examined by Folly and her legion of lies. Christ is also our defense. We need not be moved.

But eloquent wisdom also knows when to break the embargo.

Again the high priest questioned him, "Are you the Messiah, the Son of the Blessed One?" "I am," said Jesus, "and you will see the Son of Man seated at the right hand of Power and coming with the clouds of heaven." (Mark 14:61–65)

I AM, the Son of God replies, with the full force of every prophecy, every Scripture, every moment in history and each that is to come, every creed of affirmation that contains the ancient story. The full force of Trinitarian communion since the foundation of the world, contained and concentrated into one small phrase: I AM.

This . . . is eloquent silence.

54

FOOLISH GALATIANS

You foolish Galatians! Who has cast a spell on you, before whose eyes Jesus Christ was publicly portrayed as crucified? I only want to learn this from you: Did you receive the Spirit by the works of the law or by believing what you heard? Are you so foolish? After beginning by the Spirit, are you now finishing by the flesh? Did you experience so much for nothing—if in fact it was for nothing? (Gal. 3:1–4)

Oh, the heartbreak of seeing Wisdom-dwellers return to the house of Folly.

In our modern day, Paul's letter to the Galatians would be like that phone call we all dread to make, or perhaps the coffee date we've been avoiding for a bit too long. Like the parent who knows "this is going to hurt me more than it hurts you," we know these talks are for everybody's good, but nothing feels good about it at the time.

Louis Armstrong used to say that life had a booty-shaped paddle, especially shaped to the exact specifications for every spanking that discipline needed to give.

The apostle Paul has been sent to the people of Galatia with just such a paddle to apply, as our old country folk used to say, the "board of education to the seat of the problem."

He comes with grace and peace, but also with the paddle of truth. The Galatians were eyewitnesses to the power of the life, death, and resurrection of Christ. They saw Wisdom firsthand, and perhaps some of them had even touched and spoken with Christ directly.

But their eyes did not believe what they saw. Like children obsessed with the next shiny bit of excitement in our own modern, consumeristic society, they fell prey to Folly's enchantments. Maybe the threats from outsiders became too great for them to bear, as Folly-dwellers began to hunt and punish those who named Christ's name. With hostility increasing in the region, the good gospel seed had fallen on fertile ground, but was choked out by concern of how to live this new life and unlearn the ways of the old. The world shamed them for moving to the house of Wisdom and life, and a false teacher captivated them and persuaded that the good path was the wrong path, that they should follow another way instead. The same old serpent who distorted Wisdom's truth in the garden sent Folly once again to twist the truth of Christ.

The anger of a shepherd rose up in Paul, and he was shocked by the speed of their rejection, at their turning aside to a false teacher and a false gospel. The Galatians had fallen for the age-old lie, their hearts were darkened, and they became Folly's fools.

> Don't be deceived: God is not mocked. For whatever a person sows he will also reap, because the one who sows to his flesh will reap destruction from the flesh, but the one who sows to the Spirit will reap eternal life from the Spirit. Let us not get tired of doing good, for we will reap at the proper time if we don't give up. Therefore, as we have opportunity, let us work for the good of all, especially for those who belong to the household of faith. (Gal. 6:7–10)

But we cannot abandon bad soil to become a vacant lot. We ask the Spirit to till and treat that soil once again and drop in the gospel seed when the soil is right.

And we do not grow weary in such well-doing.

55

THE WEARY
BLUES

Don't be deceived: God is not mocked.
For whatever a person sows he will also reap.

GALATIANS 6:7

Moving in the soil of foolishness and flesh will wear us out, especially if we are trying to keep one foot in the house of Wisdom.

Langston Hughes, the great poet laureate of America's Harlem Renaissance, wrote of a deep kind of blues, the kind that comes from working for nothing. He sang of an old man slumped over this Harlem piano bench:

> Thump, thump, thump, went his foot on the floor.
> He played a few chords then he sang some more—
> "I got the Weary Blues
> And I can't be satisfied.
> Got the Weary Blues
> And can't be satisfied—
> I ain't happy no mo'
> And I wish that I had died."
> And far into the night he crooned that tune.
> The stars went out and so did the moon.
> The singer stopped playing and went to bed
> While the Weary Blues echoed through his head.
> He slept like a rock or a man that's dead.[1]

---

1. Langston Hughes, "The Weary Blues," in *The Collected Works of Langston Hughes*. Copyright © 2002 by Langston Hughes. Reprinted by permission of Harold Ober Associates, Inc. Public Domain.

6

When our soil is bad, we grow odd things. We toil in our own strength, ministering and living without Wisdom's guidance and the Spirit's power. We risk catching a case of the weary blues if we don't turn around.

Those foolish Galatians were bewitched by a different gospel than the gospel of truth and life. They turned aside perhaps to an easier gospel, one that compromised their uniqueness in Christ, which in turn compromised their Christian identity.

This other gospel perhaps returned some to the old ways of Judaism, and perhaps others to the old ways of paganism. In an age of rising hostility, it allowed them to hide and deny who they were, while the rest of the church was exposed and horribly mistreated by the same foolish and hostile culture they resisted.

Their compromise with their surrounding culture and the surrender of their unique identity turned their suffering into a twisted and perverted Passover, where the angel of death and suffering would pass over their door to visit the members of the true church. Imagine being Paul who says he "bears the marks of serving Christ on his body," writing to this church who is using this alternate gospel as protection from the whip.

What kind of soil are we cultivating in the tin ecosystems of our hearts? What will the seeds of life find? Soil of flesh or Spirit? Soil of Adam or Christ? Soil of Wisdom, or Folly that chokes and stunts?

The gardens of our souls have no borders, and bad soil can blow atop good at any time. As we disciple people and entire cultures into Wisdom, we look for rich soil that will resist pernicious ideas in favor of the soil that will bear fruit to defy Folly's world. Folly-dwellers don't even realize they hunger for better soil.

Rather, let's tend our gardens well. Mind the soil and the seeds, the predators and the protectors. Weary blues over bad soil are never far from any of us; watch, or it will overtake us like weeds in a field.

56

AN
OVER-THE-SHOULDER
GLANCE

The sun had risen over the land when Lot reached Zoar.
Then out of the sky the LORD rained on Sodom and Gomorrah
burning sulfur from the LORD. He demolished these cities,
the entire plain, all the inhabitants of the cities, and whatever grew
on the ground. But Lot's wife looked back and became
a pillar of salt. (Gen. 19:23–26)

You have heard much preaching and have become an ardent and
enthusiastic believer. But if we could imagine such a thing, there
are times when we miss the familiarity of Folly's voice: and when we
hear her call, we perk up, and forget.

Her voice appears usually when times have grown hard. The shift
from comfort with Yahweh to discomfort happened ever so gradually.
This way of obedience and following Yahweh, of "following the Wisdom of the universe," suddenly became full of risk, uncertainty, even
doubt. Perhaps it's grown difficult to be a genuine Christian in your culture, with people more openly hostile toward the biblical God in you;
the idols of the past start to look safe again. We forget their whims, their
capricious nature, their lies, their abuse.

And so, like Mother Lot, rather than seeing the lie and the destruction, we look back with blind longing at what was, and we think of what
might have been if we had just given Folly one more chance.

The old identities may not be safe, but they are familiar. In the
New Testament, following Christ uncompromisingly didn't seem to
be bringing opportunities in the short run. As it often does for Christ

followers still, it seemed to be taking them away.

Following Wisdom was—and still is—job losses and loss of income. Lot's wife longed for the wealth that salt production in Sodom and Gomorrah brought to make the city thrive. She revealed where her heart lay, and she became what she worshiped.

Closed doors. Unpopularity. Being society's "byword." Being thrown by your family into the street, exposed to those who wield their civil religion like a club or a sword.

But when Wisdom calls, we must pack our things and go. When Wisdom sends, we must ask where. Fear, longing, and blindness take away our power to persevere.

When Wisdom speaks we must listen . . .

Or else have our idols exposed.

57

SAUL ON THE
STRAIGHT STREET

Meanwhile, Saul was uttering threats with every breath and was eager to kill the Lord's followers. So he went to the high priest. He requested letters addressed to the synagogues in Damascus, asking for their cooperation in the arrest of any followers of the Way he found there. He wanted to bring them—both men and women—back to Jerusalem in chains. (Acts 9:1–2 NLT)

The mind's eye can see this very determined man, religious robes flying in the dust and wind, his face hardened as fearful servant eyes darted around him. So much anger, so much self-righteousness, so much power. The only thing that can interrupt his stride is the blinding light of Wisdom, searing white hot into his brain and bringing his ego to its knees.

Light, voice, power—the same combination that brought everything into existence—now called Saul by name. It must have been a fearsome thing, to be interrupted so.

On the dusty road to Damascus, Paul, robed in murderous pride and envy, heard Wisdom's call. He oversaw many executions like Stephen's, the faithful follower who was a more true Jew in Christ than Paul's pedigreed lineage could ever make him to be.

He who once was blinded by his own righteous zeal is now blinded by Righteousness Himself, and the puffed-up law-keeper is brought low by the Law-Fulfiller. Saul, who postured lineage, education, and knowledge, is now enlightened and enlivened by true Wisdom.

Paul has no choice but to receive Wisdom's call and learns quickly who is the King of glory.

"I am Jesus, the one you are persecuting! Now get up and go into the city, and you will be told what you must do." (Acts 9:5–6 NLT)

Struck with a divine blindness designed to yield divine sight, for three days Paul is dependent on the body of Christ and the voice of Wisdom to guide him in the Way. A life once committed to sniffing out the people of God, to binding Christ's body in chains, yields at once to a life committed to love and peace. Hate is transformed, and God struck Paul with a blindness that allowed him to truly see for the first time. His was a blindness that revealed his absolute and utter dependence on God, as well as on His people whom he had reviled and who must now learn to trust and welcome him.

And what does Paul's divine blindness reveal? The untimely born apostle is led to a house on the street ironically named Straight. He is fed by Christ's hands through a believer named Judas. He is ministered to and taught by the mouths and hearts of the believers in Damascus. The arms of the godly man Ananias enfold Paul to baptize him into new life; he no longer calls him "murderer," but calls him "brother." Paul joins the feet of Barnabas, walking the steps of joyful suffering and martyrdom and shedding his notorious reputation with each new step in Christ.

Hands that feed, mouths that proclaim, arms that enfold, feet that move, hearts that welcome. This was Christ's body making a house of wisdom and life shaped just for the apostle Paul.

He sees, finally, the oneness of the body of Christ through His people, made one in Christ. The very ones he maltreated, the One and the same he once scourged.

Could the thorn in his flesh have been the lives of those abused and crushed with his crazed passion of self-righteous religion? He thought he could please God as the chief of Pharisees but proved himself as chief of sinners; a long-time resident of Folly's house of destruction enlightened by the bright light of Wisdom on a desert road.

In a flash of marvelous, life-altering understanding, wisdom reveals to all who walk wisdom's roads the spiritual sight that sees Christ as He truly is.

58

WISDOM'S
"DUE SEASON"

Folly is known to rush about with impatience; Wisdom moves "in due season" if we don't give up. Folly wants to be seen for her deeds; Wisdom waits for recognition.

Earthly kingdom building can happen rather quickly, motivated by human effort for worldly goals that satisfy self. But waiting for results and fruit in the kingdom of God on earth takes much more time, and often requires a supernatural patience.

Whether it's simply raising godly and wise children, earning the next career promotion, seeing our communities turn from death to life, or even to cultivating humane and civil societies, attempting these good and lofty goals in our own strength will either see us falter altogether in exhaustion, or expose our many mistakes and shortcuts made along the way.

Folly's idea of success has two sides. One side is marked by impatience in being noticed. Those who seek platform over principle, who find themselves too quickly promoted to parenting, planning, or preaching without much maturing. Wisdom's side is marked by being overlooked. Those who *sowed in the Spirit* yet put principle over platform, yet who may find themselves overlooked year after year after year until their work is recognized in God's timing.

Around the globe, celebrity culture and internet fame have conditioned us to expect microwaveable ministries and foolishly built houses. The shoddy work of expediency is quickly revealed when Folly's swift work emerges. Yet Wisdom's discerning eye can detect the holes in the teaching of an unproven life; zeal is too transparent to cover extreme lack of knowledge and unpreparedness.

Wisdom takes her time and does not compromise her development.

She yields to correction as she builds and pays painstaking attention to details. Wisdom builds slowly, quietly, and after the pattern of the master craftsman, and builds her home on His solid rock.

Can we learn to spot the differences in our microwave society? Can we learn to wait?

Discipleship and culture shaping are long communal walks in the same direction, so is well-doing. Success and recognition are often long delayed, if they ever appear at all. There is an impatience that comes with a lack of recognition, but we take heart. Our names, stories, and deeds are written in the Lamb's Book of Life. Each of our names is a chapter—a story—in Wisdom's larger story of redemption.

> He will repay each one according to his works: eternal life to
> those who by persistence in doing good seek glory, honor, and
> immortality; but wrath and anger to those who are self-seeking
> and disobey the truth while obeying unrighteousness. There will
> be affliction and distress for every human being who does evil, first
> to the Jew, and also to the Greek; but glory, honor, and peace for
> everyone who does what is good, first to the Jew, and also to the
> Greek. For there is no favoritism with God. (Rom. 2:6–11)

Certainly our works on earth do not gain us eternal life, since we have been saved by grace through faith as God's good and merciful gift. However, we are commanded to live and build according to the wisdom, character, and mission of God. Whether it's speaking into an individual's life, or speaking into the culture, the first and loudest voice out of the gate may well be the voice of Folly, but the voice built on Wisdom will be the one that lasts.

God sees, guides, directs, and even times our good and worshipful building.

We cannot give up on His wisdom.

59

BAMBOO
SHOOTS

Jesus came near and said to them, "All authority has been given
to me in heaven and on earth. Go, therefore, and make disciples
of all nations, baptizing them in the name of the Father and of
the Son and of the Holy Spirit, teaching them to observe everything I have commanded you. And remember, I am with you
always, to the end of the age." (Matt. 28:18–20)

While a soul's movement from unbelief to belief can be sudden,
the movement from folly to wisdom is a process of "unlearning"
for many of us and takes time to learn Wisdom's ways.

If we have lived for a long time—perhaps a lifetime—in Folly's
house, we are very knowledgeable of the customs of her home. Destruction, self, chaos, and death have been our norm; the quiet life without
chaos feels loud to our new ears. Learning the language of wisdom and
life, and even preferring wisdom's ways, are badges of a new world that
take time to develop.

And so we wander through Wisdom's home like a bull in a china
shop, knocking and tipping and breaking and spilling. How clumsy we
are in Wisdom's world! Wisdom's companions smile, teach us to clear
the mess we've made, and then show us the better way to live.

Feeling truly comfortable in Wisdom's home, despite her grace and
warm welcome, can feel like it's taking forever.

Each new believer's growth starts as the tiniest Chinese bamboo
shoot, and the bamboo tree doesn't grow like other trees. While most
trees grow steadily over a period of years, the Chinese bamboo tree
doesn't break through the ground for the first four years. Then, in the
fifth year, the tree begins to grow at an astonishing rate. In fact, in a period

of just five weeks, a Chinese bamboo tree can grow to a height of ninety feet, and stretch out wide, hosting new life of its own. We see the sudden growth and are amazed at how beautiful, how lush, how tall.

Men and women who walk with new Wisdom-dwellers and are blessed with patience and grace in this one-step-forward, two-steps-back process will reap the harvest if they do not give up. They will marvel at the fruit in due season, as they trust in Wisdom Himself to give the increase.

In our desperate global times, we need men and women of grace, patience, and endurance; long-time Wisdom-dwellers who will persevere in speaking truth that teaches life and transformation to everyone who comes to live in Wisdom's house and find that Wisdom Himself is there.

If the field is hard, let the work be beautiful and steady, faithful in even the smallest of things; the messes and the cleanings and the learning, together. Better small things filled with the life of Christ, than the large things filled with the stench of death and self.

60

THE HOUSEHOLD
OF FAITH

One of the apostle Paul's spiritual prescriptions for enduring hostility was persevering in community. Wisdom's house is, after all, a household with attendants who are living, working, eating, resting, and learning, and doing it together.

Wisdom's home is the word-picture re-creation of the first garden home, where Adam and Eve represent not only the first marriage, and not just the first family, but also the first worshiping community. Until the serpent arrives, they are a vibrant-colored pastoral painting of contentment and provision, a world of "very good" in perfect and undisturbed communion with their Creator. All they need is there, and their Creator is all they need until Folly shatters their shalom with their own discontent.

Adam and Eve did not prefer God, and therefore they did not prefer or protect each other. Yet in the house that Christ has built called the church, consideration of the other is woven into every tapestry, every rug, sheet, and curtain. It's supposed to be the fabric of our lives.

Let the one who is taught the word share all his good things with the teacher. Don't be deceived: God is not mocked. For whatever a person sows he will also reap, because the one who sows to his flesh will reap destruction from the flesh, but the one who sows to the Spirit will reap eternal life from the Spirit. Let us not get tired of doing good, for we will reap at the proper time if we don't give up. Therefore, as we have opportunity, let us work for the good of all, especially for those who belong to the household of faith. (Gal. 6:6–10)

Paul reminds us that the seed-bed of well-doing, the place where our thoughts are refined and tested and tried, is in the community of Christ as members of His body. We shouldn't let the focus inward fool us, bearing one another's burdens and preferring the household of faith doesn't turn us into a holy huddle, where everyone in the church is facing inward and avoiding the world outside. It is, rather, a turning inward to the source of all Wisdom, Christ Himself, in our union with Him, to minister to each other, tend to each other's wounds made inside and outside of the church, and to be strengthened to once again face outward to find other wisdom seekers among the foolish. As long as we stand together and face both inward and outward, we are being salt and light to each other, and to the culture around us.

Especially to "those who belong to the household of faith." Why the priority? In the Galatians' context of hardship and persecution, they weren't getting much love from the outside world. Families sometimes cast out believers. They really only had each other.

Sometimes in our zeal for finding others, we give our best to the people outside of the household of faith. Why does our good brother Paul prioritize us? Because we are one, we should grieve the very idea of functioning one without the other, because the household of faith needs one another's strength the most.

61

THE WISER
GALATIANS

So many of the Bible's letters contained rebukes, either from one church to another, from one apostle to another, or from an apostle to the churches. Yet they were never written without encouragement or hope that the recipients could find themselves once again on the good foot in Wisdom's house. Don't we want to assume some of the churches pulled themselves together and heeded even the most difficult rebukes? There were even repentant believers among the "foolish Galatians" Paul had challenged, who had turned aside to a false gospel and returned to Folly's house for a time. For a time, they followed a gospel that compromised their uniqueness of being in Christ, which in turn compromised their Christian identity. We see the repentant ones in Peter's first letter. Some of them are among those named as exiles scattered, like good seeds, in the dispersion that was caused by increasing persecution.

> To those chosen, living as exiles dispersed abroad in Pontus, Galatia, Cappadocia, Asia, and Bithynia, chosen according to the foreknowledge of God the Father, through the sanctifying work of the Spirit, to be obedient and to be sprinkled with the blood of Jesus Christ. May grace and peace be multiplied to you.
> (1 Peter 1:1–2)

It seems that they found their way back to wisdom's ways, because they're being encouraged to stay strong in the midst of hostility and they are named among the obedient. There's hope in their journey here for all wayward Christians! They conquered their fears of being known as Christ followers and identified themselves by His name enough to need encouragement to hang on and weather the storm.

Their repentance invites us to consider what kinds of seeds we are scattering as we travel the town beyond wisdom's door. Scattering seeds of wisdom, or folly? Seeds of self-reliance, or seeds of dependence on the Spirit? Seeds of beauty or deformity? Seeds of community or isolation? Seeds that will cause our culture to flourish or to wither?

And more importantly, seeds that will cause the household of faith to flourish, or cause her to wither?

If we are casting good seeds from wisdom's garden around our towns, we will receive blowback from those who hate wisdom and love death. It is assured.

> The world hated them because they are not of the world, just as I am not of the world. I am not praying that you take them out of the world but that you protect them from the evil one. They are not of the world, just as I am not of the world. Sanctify them by the truth; your word is truth. As you sent me into the world, I also have sent them into the world. I sanctify myself for them, so that they also may be sanctified by the truth. (John 17:14–19)

Christ wastes nothing; He uses even our failings and our genuine repentance as a part of our sanctification by the truth. And having been restored from and delivered from the house of Folly once again, we have the scars that remind us to keep our hearts close to home and let them abide in our only true shelter, even as we go about. It's dangerous out there.

> *Jesus is a Rock in a weary land.*
> *A weary Land, a weary land*
> *Jesus is a Rock in a weary land,*
> *A Shelter in the Time of Storm.*[1]

---

1. An early printed version of this spiritual appears in *A Collection of Revival Hymns and Plantation Melodies* (Cincinnati, OH: 1883), compiled by African American Methodist Episcopal minister Marshall W. Taylor (1846–1887). There have been many arrangements and stanza versions since its first notation.

62

HEALED TO
THE BONE

When we seek wisdom, we seek Christ Himself. We can seek to live the life that He set out for us, or we can go our own way.

Just like our first parents in the garden, we have two possible positions: folly or wisdom.

One way leads to death, the other to life.

The contrast between wise and foolish choices, and the consequences of each and the quality of peace we experience based on what we choose, is laced throughout Scripture. In fact, it seems almost every choice made by any of our scriptural ancestors, in any point in history, is a choice between wisdom that leads to life and folly that leads to death.

The book of Proverbs prepares us for this truth and blesses us with a hard dose of reality—the personal consequences of seeking wisdom over folly. Keep the events of the garden account in mind as you read these verses, as they seem to drip with knowledge and regret over what was lost:

> Trust in the LORD with all your heart, and do not rely on your own understanding;
>
> in all your ways know him, and he will make your paths straight.
>
> Don't be wise in your own eyes; fear the LORD and turn away from evil.
>
> This will be healing for your body and strengthening for your bones. (Prov. 3:5–8)

And yet the benefits of heeding Wisdom's call go beyond mere life choices—it is a call of even greater consequences than escaping personal pain. It is the call from death to new life in Christ. Wisdom's voice is His, standing atop the high place of Mount Sinai teaching Israel life from death, and claiming freedom from that death into new life on Golgotha's hill.

Wisdom calls us not to mere moralism, but to newness, and escape from the senselessness and tyranny of the world of folly and destruction, death and the grave.

Come unto me, Wisdom cries! It is finished, the Savior cries! Come unto Me, all who labor, and I will give you rest—rest and peace to your soul.

From the highest heights to the lowest depths . . . come into Wisdom's house, and rest.

63

DIVINELY
DEFINED

Do you not know? Have you not heard?
The LORD is the everlasting God, the Creator of
the whole earth. He never becomes faint or weary;
there is no limit to his understanding.

ISAIAH 40:28

The King of Glory is great, and greatly to be praised. Psalmist and prophet alike call this wise King unsearchable. Even so, Scripture plumbs the unknowable perfections of His character and His nature; no one can exhaust its depths; like a hyperdimensional cube—a tesseract— that both exists across time and space yet also defies their laws, there are just too may refractions of His knowledge, wisdom, justice, and grace to catch with the human mind; of His greatness there is no end.

But there are limits to ours.

The kingdom people are defined by the character of their King. The subjects of a good leader of an organization, institution, military, nation, or family will carry their head's reputation and nature with them as they visit other principalities. So as we leave Wisdom's house and travel about the world, we do carry Wisdom Himself, marked in our own distinctive way that is suited to our human nature, yet also very different from the wisdom of men.

There is a knowledge and a wisdom that comes from Folly's house, but it is a grace and a gift from God—borrowed from Wisdom's house so that our homes, lives, and streets can remain, at the very least, civil and humane. By this borrowed wisdom Folly can at times seem quite wise. But because Folly refuses to bend her knee to true Wisdom, the apostle Paul tells us that this wisdom of the age, be they sage teachers, skilled scientists, generous philanthropists, or even ethical politicians, will ultimately come to nothing lasting beyond this life. Since she cannot enter eternity if she doesn't recognize ultimate Wisdom, then a borrowed wisdom is all the wisdom that Folly will ever know.

Those who are seasoned in Christ—those who have simmered long and suffered the difficulties and placed their hope and knowledge in Wisdom Himself, know the wisdom that lasts and builds things that no eye has seen or ear heard as yet. Like Jules Verne's explorers journeying to the center of the earth, passing the strata of civilization to find untold wonders and treasure, the Spirit of God began this journey of discernment and revelation from the foundation of the world. The Wisdom from above has seen the Spirit search its depths in its journey to the center of our hearts, to our intentions, and infused them with a desire for God's will. And He waits patiently until Wisdom calls and quickens the heart to know that there is much more beyond this world than anything the human eye can see.

Precious gift, this mind of Christ that sees beyond the temporal into the eternal with the eyes of faith and the heart of patience. Just a little while longer, beloved, and all will be made plain.

> For who has known the Lord's mind,
> that he may instruct him?
> But we have the mind of Christ.
> (1 Cor. 2:16)

Wisdom-dwellers apprehend God's wisdom by His Spirit; it is an in-house affair. Folly-dwellers can never understand the secret joys of the cross or the way of redemption, unless they cross into Wisdom's house. And though not even Christ's own will know Him exhaustively, in His mercy He has made it so we can know Him truly.

And that, of course, is the wisdom we most need.

64

DEEDS VS. MISDEEDS:
THE NEXT GENERATION

> One generation will declare your works to the next and will pro-
> claim your mighty acts.
> I will speak of your splendor and glorious majesty and your won-
> drous works.
> They will proclaim the power of your awe-inspiring acts, and I will
> declare your greatness.· They will give a testimony of your great
> goodness and will joyfully sing of your righteousness.
> (Ps. 145:4–7)

Testimonies of Wisdom's power and guidance are *good* gossip, if there can be such a thing.

The oral tradition of giving testimony is a powerful thing. Christians in societies that rely more on oral ways of communication know that proclamation is powerful, precious, generational, and personal. Christians in the world's most challenging places cannot help but tell of God's goodness, His faithfulness in the hardest of times, and how His wisdom brought them through.

> First giving honor to God, who is the head of my life,
> I'd like to say I'm glad to be in the house of the Lord one mo' time.
> Cause he brought me from a mighty long way.
> I coulda been dead, sleeping in my grave, but God is good all the time,
> and all the time, God is good. He's a bridge over troubled waters. He's
> a mother to the motherless, and a father to the fatherless; a doctor in a
> sickroom, and a lawyer in the courtroom. He's the lily of the valley, the
> bright and morning star.

He got up early one Sunday mornin', with all power in his hand!
Pray for me that I grow STRONGER in the Lord.[1]

If we are wise, our generation that is passing away will already be equipping the next, by telling of God's great deeds; telling the ones coming into and coming up in the faith how we exercised God's wisdom and how He delivered in our day; telling them how He brought us over.

We should tell them what we heard from our faith mothers and fathers, and how they witnessed God's mighty deeds moving in and through His people in redemptive history, building a kingdom that is not of this world.

One church mother once quipped, "Without a good testimony, you'd think we were all born holy, all-knowing, and wise—we *need* to declare or we'll bust!"

We cannot leave the next generation only with man's misdeeds inside the church, and leave the greater and redemptive deeds of God unmentioned. As we tell of God's victories and deeds, we relate how His wisdom and knowledge of navigating this cold and foolish world flows into the next generations, and our children's curiosity and doubts give way to faith. We teach as we tell and proclaim.

David is telling us one way to be like Wisdom Himself is through declaring the deeds of the King whose story is unlike every other story from every other culture on earth. The one writing the story is unique, and the ones living and telling that story are unique. The one writing that story is also fulfilling it.

No other culture on earth has such a story.

The kingdom line, from Genesis to Revelation, has extended its whispers and shouts of God's mighty deeds through history to us today.

And what should we declare?

His mighty acts. His wondrous works. His wisdom, glory, power, and fame.

And as we tell, we strengthen faith of the next generation of Wisdom's house.

---

1. You won't find this well-known piece published anywhere. It's a part of oral tradition and has been around for many, many years. I have started reciting this in conferences, and every African American in the audience says it right along with me, leaving the other folks rather perplexed!

65

ROCK IN A
WEARY LAND

T ucked into a listing of warriors of David is a remarkable phrase describing one group. "The Issacharites, who understood the times" (1 Chron. 12:32). Another version says it this way: "Issachar, men who had understanding of the times" (ESV).

Deborah (name has been changed) and her work bring to mind the word "firebrand." In wisdom, like the Issacharites, she understands where she lives, why she is there, and what she should do.

Deborah lives among an unreached people group. Long ago, they were stripped of their dignity, identity, and God-given purpose in life. Grave injustices have brought this entire population to a place where there is no electricity or water. There are very few economic opportunities, and hope is in short supply.

Everything around them is the color of sand. Time passes very slowly in this arid place, barren and unyielding. After generations of dehumanizing conditions, her people's outlook had grown understandably bleak. They were filled with despair that they'd been forgotten by the rest of the world.

Yet Deborah has this intense flair for the creative, and a deep love for her people. Every day, she tries to answer one question: "Until justice is served, how will we live?" Holy Spirit–ingenuity has proven to be her greatest weapon against the despair that always hovers over their heads.

With a warrior's spirit, Deborah has decided that circumstances won't win. She battles their despair by creating programs that are energizing her people. The youngest children are now being equipped with educational programs that paint their desert with the color and beauty of a practical love. Once, when presented with a request for baptism, she solved the lack of water with a trip to a community shower. There is always a creative way to navigate every obstacle.

Year in and year out, her actions, wisdom, and ingenuity say, "God sees you. I see you. You matter."

Deborah and her people are blooming in the desert, and seeing their dignity restored. Her wisdom and creativity, poured out on her by the Holy Spirit, is restoring their humanity one idea at a time, one day at a time, one person at a time, one generation at a time.

She's the "least of these" among the "least of these" . . . and they're beautiful. This is modern-day perseverance in the face of injustice. Through wisdom in the moment and hope in the future. They have set up a tent of wisdom in a barren land.

Until justice comes, they fight, they love. And they flourish.

Like a lily in the valley, she lives.

> I've found a friend in Jesus, He's everything to me,
> He's the fairest of ten thousand to my soul;
> The Apple-tree of trees, in Him alone I see
> All I need to cleanse and make me fully whole.
> In sorrow He's my comfort, in trouble He's my stay,
> He tells me every care on Him to roll:
> He's the Apple-tree of trees, the Bright and Morning Star,
> He's the fairest of ten thousand to my soul.
> —William Charles Fry (1837–1882)

Here is this hymn as Deborah and her community sing it in their language:

> *Mo ti ni Jesu lore, O j'ohun gbogbo fun mi*
> *Oun nikan larewa ti okan mi fe, Oun nitanna ipado*
> *Oun ni Enikan naa, To le we mi nu kuro nin'ese mi*
> *Olutunu mi lo je ni gbogbo wahala, Oun ni ki n kaniyan mi l'Oun lori*
> *Oun n'Itanna Ipado,Irawo Owuro*
> *Oun nikan l'Arewa ti okan mi fe.*

66

WISDOM AT WATCHNIGHT

But God understands the way to wisdom,
and he knows its location.
For he looks to the ends of the earth
and sees everything under the heavens.
When God fixed the weight of the wind
and distributed the water by measure,
when he established a limit for the rain
and a path for the lightning,
he considered wisdom and evaluated it;
he established it and examined it.
He said to mankind,
"The fear of the LORD—that is wisdom.
And to turn from evil is understanding." (Job 28:23–28)

Older saints who have been through the university of life are a blessing to the body of Christ. They already know that life on its own is hard and profoundly disappointing, but they can rest in the knowledge that life with Christ is also difficult—but blessed.

One older saint named Mother Marie had buried two adult children in tragic circumstances. Well into her eighties, she would sing and cry from her honored first soprano seat high in the choir loft. Her tears were moved by her faith in God's wisdom behind her losses, moved by His ability to redeem what death seemed to have stolen.

Now deceased herself, Mother Marie's voice still rings in many memories, like those Sunday morning chapel bells of God's faithfulness in the midst of tragedy. While she moaned in that choir loft, she praised and poured out her heart to the one true God who is good and great in a broken and hateful world. She sang the glory of the promised, unshakable kingdom down until it enveloped and comforted her like a divine blanket, and it gave her strength to carry on. She had learned with each of life's pains that there was no comfort in Folly's house; Folly was short on maternal instinct and had no compassion that would scoop up the hurting and rock them with nurture and care necessary for that depth of grief.

Wisdom's house is the only place to go to heal a heart broken by a sin-sick world.

Old saints will know of meeting Wisdom at their New Year's Watchnight services that saw scores of black folks' voices raised against the rafters became still as a hush; a lone voice calls to the Watchman: "Watchman, watchman, please tell me the hour!"[1]

As the Watchman called out the time moment by moment, the faithful watched the old year expire and reflected on how good God had been in the wicked chaos of folly. It was a time of confession, repentance, anticipation, wisdom, strengthening, and peace.

And those who heard Wisdom's call to step into the household of faith learned why they stayed so late and sang so long on those watchnights; because when the King of all wisdom is present, bringing comfort to the hurting, He is well worth staying long for.

Because the King of wisdom is unshakable in a world that too often leaves us shaken and shocked in its darkness. We need the unshakable wisdom, the penetrating light, and the everlasting arms of our unshakable King.

---

1. Editors of *Encyclopaedia Britannica*, "Watch Night," last updated January 5, 2023, https://www.britannica.com/topic/Watch-Night.

67

ULTIMATE, UNSHAKABLE WISDOM

> His voice shook the earth at that time, but now he has prom-
> ised, Yet once more I will shake not only the earth but also
> the heavens. This expression, "Yet once more," indicates the
> removal of what can be shaken—that is, created things—so
> that what is not shaken might remain. Therefore, since we are
> receiving a kingdom that cannot be shaken, let us be thankful.
> By it, we may serve God acceptably, with reverence and awe, for
> our God is a consuming fire. (Heb. 12:26–29)

Once we are one with the King and safely stowed in Wisdom's house, we are no longer a part of a shakable earthly kingdom; we are now part of the everlasting kingdom that shakes the earth.

The kingdom of God doesn't come with our careful branding, our public proclamations, news articles, powerful speeches, cultivated social media management, or strategic movement shaping. Those things have their place, and God will judge the effectiveness and wisdom of them all. That is, by and large, all earthly business.

God's kingdom is far more likely to come from among the unpopular, unlikely, unknown, and unheard; from among those engaged in the daily grind and who are faithfully bringing light to the shadows. Just as Christ came to this burdened, darkened world. Those humble enough to admit that their arms alone are too weak to shake anything temporal or eternal.

The names of ordinary people mark the book of Acts far more impressively than the names of kings, rulers, and culture shapers.

The earth is the one who is shaken. It is shaken through the King's quiet intrusion as a baby, born far away from prying eyes, at the moment when everyone is looking for a king to establish a new political rule, a prophet to deliver a long-waited word from God after much silence, or a priest to move.

This King has surprised the world with an unshakable kingdom that brings the world a different kind of politics—not antipolitical; not a rejection of culture—it's living an "other culture" altogether. It's a politics based on the life, death, and resurrection of Jesus Christ. It is based on Him, and the realities of creation, fall, redemption, and glory. Wisdom has arrived on the scene as the subject and content of His own story as Prophet, Priest, and King arriving as one.

We were literally created to inhabit Wisdom's story, and it's Wisdom's story, embedded in the universe, that sets us apart from Folly's. Our identity, our story of the fulfillment of promises in Wisdom's perfect timing and with its nature-defying details; this story will determine our priorities and set us free as members of the unshakable kingdom.

Earthly politics: important, but not ultimate.

History and social movements: important, but not ultimate.

Nations, tongues, and tribes: important, but not ultimate.

Christ and the wisdom of His kingdom: *ultimate.*

God is still making a holy nation of His own, a people for Himself. This kingdom isn't shakable, but rather shakes everything around it. Moreover, it shakes us in a proud way, by the wisdom and deeds of the great King we serve . . . and we are to remain steadfast because our foundation is in Him.

68

HOMECOMING

Those who prefer Folly's house in the here and now will never experience any more than what this world holds. But what awaits Wisdom-dwellers in the sweet by-and-by, even as we live in today's nasty now-and-now?

Nothing short of a true homecoming.

The three basic blessings that Folly stole in Eden will become a glorified reality. Revelation gives us the full view of what the psalmists are singing and shouting and clapping about.

We are no longer just a garden, or a well-tended home that Wisdom has made; there's a whole new city in view. We don't just *receive* a new dwelling place. The invisible church that spans time and language *is* the new City.

> Then I saw a new heaven and a new earth; for the first heaven and the first earth had passed away, and the sea was no more. I also saw the holy city, the new Jerusalem, coming down out of heaven from God, prepared like a bride adorned for her husband.
>
> Then I heard a loud voice from the throne: Look, God's dwelling is with humanity, and he will live with them. They will be his peoples, and God himself will be with them and will be their God. He will wipe away every tear from their eyes. Death will be no more; grief, crying, and pain will be no more, because the previous things have passed away. (Rev. 21:1–4)

Justice and mercy are dispensed in perfect measure. Folly's bombs, abuses, her liars, cheaters, swindlers, the death, pain, perversion, and tears she wrought? All gone with the garden's serpent, now a full-blown dragon tormenting the nations; he is cast into the lake of fire and his judgment has come. The threat to security is gone, and no unclean or accursed thing will ever enter its fortified walls again.

The house where we will dwell with Wisdom Himself is now a perfect nation, with no government bureaucracy, red tape, or corruption. God's government that rests upon His shoulders will be established as the new heavens and new earth.

How good it will be to come Home.

Our new Home is grand, opulent even. Protected and fortified with high and strong walls, it is the ultimate safety. It's the place He's gone to prepare for us, just as He lovingly crafted and prepared a place for us at creation.

Inside its fortified walls, true Wisdom has set out the banqueting table, and has saved us a seat. Just as in Proverbs 8, and those who answered Wisdom's call will take their seats at the Lamb's supper. We can finally eat from the Tree of Life whose leaves heal the wounds of the nations. We have Communion with Christ, in glorified flesh and blood, gathering the ones whom Wisdom called to sup. His outstretched, nail-scarred hands remind us He has longed to share this meal with us on the victory side, where Folly's call is no longer heard, and enter Wisdom's house by and through the Lamb.

This kingdom comes as His will is done, and the King of wisdom holds each place as He calls.

69

RECLINING AT WISDOM'S TABLE

We "good" people are filled with poor excuses. A host sends out invitations and assures all guests that a spot has been made *just for them* at his table, in her home, or in our congregations. We trust that the invitation itself will prove that they are wanted in the prepared spot, and if the invitation isn't reassurance enough, we tell them with our words: *There is a place here for you; you are wanted here!*

Yet deep in our hearts on the receiving side, we are convinced that there must be some mistake, and so we reach into our box of handy excuses. Or perhaps we don't even show up at all. At the critical moment when all the guests have gathered, the banquet is perfectly timed and laid out on the feasting table and the host opens his arms in welcome— there is a glaring spot open, made vacant by excuse and priority. And thus, we play out in daily life the scene our Lord describes to us in Scripture of the reality of His invitation, and what He will do when excuses are made: "Go out into the highways and hedges and make them come in, so that my house may be filled. For I tell you, not one of those people who were invited will enjoy my banquet" (Luke 14:22–24).

Of the many truths He assures us in this passage, one stands out: He will fill His house with His own. Although He came to "His own" called Israel and many resisted Him as Messiah, those He drew to His table found their seats and dined with the King.

The people traveling the world's highways and byways are diverse. The people of the world encompass languages, tongues, and tribes, yet they all have one thing in common: the same sin-sickness of the soul born in the garden of Eden. They also have in common Wisdom's voice calling to the great banqueting hall, yet those whose ears are only tuned to the call of Folly will present every clever reason to remain in Folly's cold, self-satisfying embrace.

The kingdom will be filled with human variety, with the promise made to Abraham long ago: that he would father a nation as vast and varied as the sands, a people blessed to be a blessing to the world around them. If you hear Wisdom's call today, do not delay your inevitable, irresistible entry into this House of Life; as has been told us for generations, you must come in by and through the Lamb.

While the Bible tells us Christ was ethnically Jewish, it also tells us that He is the true and perfect human. As He gathers the nations to Himself, He stands as the perfect African American, African, or European; the perfect Asian, Latin American, Pacific Islander, and so on, with *all* ethnicities. He issues His call in every language, so that every ear is guaranteed to hear. That's how much He longs to see us seated at His table, in communion with Him.

As Creator and Lord of the nations and the only perfect participant among them, Christ identifies with each nation with such completeness, depth, and totality that only He is able to ultimately consummate and bring them into harmony. When we answer Wisdom's call in the now, we embrace Christ's ingathering of all nations, tribes, peoples, and tongues to worship around His glorified body on the throne.

Though race and ethnicity in and of themselves are neither holy nor profane, they are our divinely designed reality and therefore they are precious gifts from our Creator Christ. But out of this many, one will come through our union with Him. When we meet Christ in glory, His kingdom will be established as the preeminent tribe, as we are made one new people. We'll receive the redemption of even our earthly identities, and marvel at the vast riches of the banqueting table with thanksgiving, reverence, and awe.

It's around this table that the invisible church is made visible, and we see that while we are many, we are truly one.

And it was Christ's wisdom that foresaw and foretold our new, perfected "very good."

70

THE FRAGRANCE
OF WISDOM

She disrupted the proceedings with her worship and her tears. A life devoted to the house of lies had left her heart overcome with sin. Some days, she didn't even recognize who she had become.

She had glimpsed Him often as she scanned the crowds, eyes veiled and head bowed. Peeping between shoulders and shadows, she stayed near the crowd's edge for a quick exit should hostility turn toward her, or even worse, lust. As she craned her neck above shoulders ahead, she heard a man speak in a way she had never heard: not of condemnation, but of forgiving sins. She knew hers were many, and those perpetrated against her were even more. The first few times it sounded improbable—she overheard the leaders interrogate the man with, "Who has authority to forgive sins?" She dismissed him as just another liar from Folly's house.

And then Wisdom bade her, seemingly called to her as if He knew her whole life, "Come child; rest, and live." Her bare and dusted feet ran home and, precious perfume box in hand, she ran to where she heard He would be.

Then one of the Pharisees invited him to eat with him. He entered the Pharisee's house and reclined at the table. And a woman in the town who was a sinner found out that Jesus was reclining at the table in the Pharisee's house. She brought an alabaster jar of perfume and stood behind him at his feet, weeping, and began to wash his feet with her tears. She wiped his feet with her hair, kissing them and anointing them with the perfume.

When the Pharisee who had invited him saw this, he said to himself, "This man, if he were a prophet, would know who and what kind of woman this is who is touching him—she's a sinner!"

Jesus replied to him, "Simon, I have something to say to you." He said, "Say it, teacher."

"A creditor had two debtors. One owed five hundred denarii, and the other fifty. Since they could not pay it back, he graciously forgave them both. So, which of them will love him more?"

Simon answered, "I suppose the one he forgave more."

"You have judged correctly," he told him. Turning to the woman, he said to Simon, "Do you see this woman? I entered your house; you gave me no water for my feet, but she, with her tears, has washed my feet and wiped them with her hair. You gave me no kiss, but she hasn't stopped kissing my feet since I came in. You didn't anoint my head with olive oil, but she has anointed my feet with perfume. Therefore I tell you, her many sins have been forgiven; that's why she loved much. But the one who is forgiven little, loves little." Then he said to her, "Your sins are forgiven."

Those who were at the table with him began to say among themselves, "Who is this man who even forgives sins?"

And he said to the woman, "Your faith has saved you. Go in peace." (Luke 7:36–50)

The greater the sinner, the greater the love. Folly had taken everything from her, except the precious perfume. More precious than the perfume, perhaps, were the kisses once reserved for others now lavished in holy fashion on the feet of the Divine.

The naysayers from the house of Folly gnashed their teeth, partly at her extravagance and partly at her indictment of them all, the foolish things of the world confounded the self-appointed wise. In seeing the Messiah as they had not, her actions accused as much as they praised.

As she faded into the night, her heart was mended and her sins forgiven. Hair saturated with His fragrance, the aroma of Wisdom drifted in her wake past her neighbors. And she was the only one in the whole entire room privileged to carry Christ's fragrance to the streets.

71

WISDOM
SPEAKS TRUTH

Who among you is wise and understanding? By his good
conduct he should show that his works are done in the
gentleness that comes from wisdom. (James 3:13)

The Bible lays out a unique story that is always worth revisiting:
A good and loving God created a people to worship Him, to enjoy harmony with fellow humans, and to cultivate the rest of creation.
That world was interrupted by sin and disobedience, which the Creator
dealt with as a sacrifice of obedience so that His relationship with His
creation could be restored and perfected. This is the good and truthful
story told and lived around the heart in the house of Wisdom, the one
we revisit each time we gather for the Lord's Supper, when we remind
ourselves and our community that this story is ours, the one to which
we belong.

There are also false stories that run counter to this story of life.
These stories are made by worshiping a false god, and they too have
eternal consequences, with the power to degrade people and turn them
into the image of the idols they promote.[1]

Wisdom's house, by its very existence, invites us to examine intentions of our hearts and reflect on which story we are following. And
Wisdom wants us to be sure, because our habits and ethics and actions
will be informed by the story. Wisdom knows that we become what we
worship. We develop the habits and characteristics of what we worship;
we take on the sounds and language of our idols, and they will prove

---

1. Brian Fikkert and Kelly Kapic, *Becoming Whole: Why the Opposite of Poverty Isn't the American Dream*
(Chicago: Moody Publishers, 2019), 51–67.

themselves by conforming us to their likeness. If they lie, we tell lies to ourselves and others.

Or we live and speak truth of the truthful ancient story, proclaiming God's goodness until He comes.

James is writing this letter to a scattered people who, on the one hand, lived more closely to the ancient story—and also to those who were living further away from it. All in the same community, the household of God, the body of faith.

> If you have bitter envy and selfish ambition in your heart, don't boast and deny the truth. Such wisdom does not come down from above but is earthly, unspiritual, demonic. For where there is envy and selfish ambition, there is disorder and every evil practice. (James 3:14–16)

This was a people under persecution; it was imperative to know that one followed the story of life and not of death. Some had watched Stephen, the earliest recorded martyr, smile heavenward as he was stoned; some of these same people had buried his battered body. They deeply feared Saul and his men, whose anti-Christian rampage spread death and destruction across their region. With prison or death assured, these people known for enduring "the great persecution" needed to be sure of Christ's story (see Acts 8:1–8).

> The wisdom from above is first pure, then peace-loving, gentle, compliant, full of mercy and good fruits, unwavering, without pretense. And the fruit of righteousness is sown in peace by those who cultivate peace. (James 3:17–18)

Who we worship defines who we are, and when we worship the one, true God, our worship marks us as God's set-apart people. Many a modern mama has sent her children out for the day reminding them, "Don't just remember who you are, remember whose you are."

Oh, may it be said of us that we sound like the Savior because we have spent time with Him, because we live in Wisdom's house, and because we are the people of His story and His alone.

72

SAY OUGHTA
MATCH DO

What we know about God should produce fruit in keeping with His character. God's wisdom chafes against the grain of Folly-dwellers and sets their teeth on edge.

If we say we follow Christ, but our actions do not line up with following Him, we are self-deceived.

"Say oughta match do . . ." Or so the old people used to tell us. They weren't talking about following Christ's wisdom as a list of moralistic dos and don'ts, but rather as the qualities needed in times of trials against the church. We will cheat ourselves if we reduce the Bible to a book of moral perfection; this is a living story about character; about our affections and whom we worship.

> But be doers of the word and not hearers only, deceiving yourselves. Because if anyone is a hearer of the word and not a doer, he is like someone looking at his own face in a mirror. For he looks at himself, goes away, and immediately forgets what kind of person he was. (James 1:22–24)

Epistemology and ethics are like two sides of a zipper. Our ethics (how we obey God; the things we do) and our epistemology (what we say we know about God) should match if we are following after Christ. "The one who looks intently into the perfect law of freedom and perseveres in it, and is not a forgetful hearer but a doer who works—this person will be blessed in what he does" (James 1:25).

So the next time you zip up your child's clothes, you can say, "Baby girl, this side is your ethics and this side is your epistemology and they are supposed to be consistent with each other, since good actions are always downstream from godly character." And if she doesn't understand all that, tell her that God wants her "say" to match her "do."

Too often, like those who received James's letter, our say (what we say we believe about God) and our do (how we obey God) Do. Not. Match.

We know that God has come to redeem a people for Himself, but we keep redefining that people according to our own disobedient likeness, our own agendas, our own priorities, our own desires.

To the pure, everything is pure, but to those who are defiled and unbelieving nothing is pure; in fact, both their mind and conscience are defiled. They claim to know God, but they deny him by their works. They are detestable, disobedient, and unfit for any good work. (Titus 1:15–16)

When we say we are of the kingdom but are more concerned with discipling others into earthly cultural, social, or political positions than discipling them into the ways of God's kingdom, we may well have an idol. When we bristle at someone else touching our idol, correcting us, commenting on it, or even pointing out our inconsistencies, we've given ourselves over to an idol. The hypocrite is an idol worshiper who is blind to his own moral inconsistency; hypocrites are fools.

The third question of the Westminster Catechism asks and answers this question straight from Scripture. "What do the Scriptures principally teach? The Scriptures principally teach what man is to believe concerning God, and what duty God requires of man."[1] In order to test if our say matches our do, we first must ask who sits on the throne of our heart.

The blindness of hypocrisy creeps in so gradually, and with such subtlety, that we must examine ourselves often. And in order for our say to match our do and avoid that trap, consider today: Does my say match my do?

---

1. Westminster Shorter Catechism, Question 3, https://www.shortercatechism.com/resources/wsc/wsc_003.html.

73

FOLLY
LOVES FEAR

Now if any of you lacks wisdom, he should ask God—who
gives to all generously and ungrudgingly—and it will be given
to him. But let him ask in faith without doubting.

JAMES 1:5-6A

We are not being told here to avoid doubting; doubt is a part of our human condition. As long as we are in our earthly bodies, shadows will appear longer than their reality and the unknown will always be faced with at least a bit of trepidation.

So nowhere are we told the doubt itself is a sin. Rather, we are told that *when we doubt*, we have a place to bring it: to the throne in faith that our concerns will be allayed and our hope assured. We are to bring it to the throne of true Wisdom, in prayer.

If left in our hands, fear makes us tighten our grip on our doubt. When we hold on to it to puzzle it out ourselves without asking Wisdom to guide our perceptions and inform our unknowns, our unchecked doubt undermines our hope and our assurance of truth. It hardens our hearts and produces rebellion. That's why "the doubter is like the surging sea, driven and tossed by the wind. That person should not expect to receive anything from the Lord, being double-minded and unstable in all his ways" (James 1:6b-8).

Doubt is one of Folly's greatest foils. Doubt run amok paves the sure road back to Folly's house. The return ticket to Folly's house is purchased with doubt and fear. We run back to the house of Folly, who holds more doubt and fear than our souls were meant to bear:

Do you see a person who is wise in his own eyes?
There is more hope for a fool than for him.
(Prov. 26:12)

We cannot soothe our own doubts well; our sight and understanding are limited. Apart from wisdom, we will rationalize our doubts, casting a pall over the good life that Wisdom provided. We ask the same question as our parents in Eden: "Can this God be trusted?"

We dare not make the God of the universe who hung our moon and stars to be a liar about His own world and word. Better to bring our doubts swiftly to Him, and He will prove to us He is just who He says He is: fully transparent, fully trustworthy, fully true.

74

FOLLY IN
DISGUISE

A mid persecution, the apostles seemed to fear hypocrisy and idolatry inside the house of God more than they feared the persecution itself.

A tried Christian is a crowned Christian. Yet in the midst of rising persecution, the apostle James is more concerned with rising fear, doubt, hypocrisy, and idolatry. "No one undergoing a trial should say, 'I am being tempted by God,'" he cautions his readers (James 1:13). We were told to expect trouble, but to take heart; so the trouble, though painful, comes as no surprise. It is the fear and doubt that Folly sows among the Wisdom-dwellers that are an even deeper concern.

Destruction from within rips the community from the inside out and would do even greater damage to the body and the witness of Christ than those who could kill the body and not the soul. James wants us, in the midst of anti-Christian hostility, to tend first to any folly in our own souls before we look at the souls of the foolish.

The people called by God's name have not always followed wisdom. Even Jesus met the religious leaders of His day and warned them that their own hypocrisy would blind them to their own inner decay. The compromise, greed, exploitation, and capitulation to the culture and politics is a deceptive cancer that rotted Judah and Israel from the inside out.

Folly often puts on its religious disguise, and infiltrates Wisdom's house, becoming more like culture than Christ. But Jesus warned them: "Woe to you, scribes and Pharisees, hypocrites! You clean the outside of the cup and dish, but inside they are full of greed and self-indulgence. Blind Pharisee! First clean the inside of the cup, so that the outside of it may also become clean" (Matt. 23:25–26). He added that they were like whitewashed tombs that have a beautiful outward appearance, but inwardly were full of dead bones. Then, "on the outside you seem righteous to people, but inside you are full of hypocrisy and lawlessness" (v. 28).

James reminds us:

Each person is tempted when he is drawn away and enticed by his own evil desire. Then after desire has conceived, it gives birth to sin, and when sin is fully grown, it gives birth to death.
(James 1:14–15)

And so goes Folly's descent into madness and crimes of exploitation and indulgence. Yet here is James, telling the beleaguered church that their greatest enemy is not without but within. The only antidote is to guard their words, their hearts, their fruit, and good works of wisdom and life; otherwise, they will compromise the very thing that sets them apart from the persecutors—the ability to reflect the very character, nature, and wisdom of God.

Energy flows where our focus goes. The life-giving Christ of the ancient story is far more powerful than death and destruction. If we are speaking death and destruction—words that spread the infection of the imposters in Wisdom's house—we've no doubt turned inward and blinded ourselves by worshiping our own satisfaction.

PARTIALITY, OR GETTING THAT GOOD SEAT

Folly loves to divide. She is not careful about how she does it. Like a Civil War surgeon operating on the battlefield, she isolates and amputates with whatever crude tools she has lying about. Her goals of dissection, destruction, and division are accomplished, but the patient suffers terribly. A spiritual version of the notoriously evil Dr. Mengele, she delights in mutilating and mangling individuals, communities, and nations alike. She cannot build. The oppressive systems she has built throughout history—colonization, racism, Nazism, Marxism, Christian nationalism, antiracism, and all global, polarizing forces even of the last two centuries that drive fratricidal battles—they all carry aspects of the gods of Folly, and will never deliver the social equality they promise.

There is no true healing or unity in Folly's world; partiality and tribalism prevent it. In Wisdom's economy, partiality is forbidden; not merely because it's morally wrong and denigrates the image of God in others, but because it's idolatry, and no idol can stand in the face of God. Idols exclude as they divide and puff up as they push down. By contrast, pure worship sacrifices and lifts up.

> My brothers and sisters, do not show favoritism as you hold on to the faith in our glorious Lord Jesus Christ. For if someone comes into your meeting wearing a gold ring and dressed in fine clothes, and a poor person dressed in filthy clothes also comes in, if you look with favor on the one wearing the fine clothes and say, "Sit here in a good place," and yet you say to the poor person, "Stand over there," or "Sit here on the floor by my footstool," haven't you made distinctions among yourselves and become judges with evil thoughts? (James 2:1–4)

We read here of the church's classism. A rich brother is getting the good seat in the assembly, while the poor brother sits on the floor. Should this cancer of favoritism spread, the whole community would give in to the idol of "status." The communal design of life in Christ means that just as blessings abound and compound in community, so do the curses from our sin. We should never think that we sin in a vacuum, as we always take others with us, and often our personal idols make communities of their own. Just as God is bent on maximum life and transformation, our idols are bent on maximum destruction and dehumanization of our souls. However, in this scene, Christ dashed Folly's partiality of earthly distinctions, categories, and cliques at the cross, declaring that they do not belong in His house where everyone is equally sinful, equally forgiven, and equally transformed at the foot of the cross:

> Listen, my dear brothers and sisters: Didn't God choose the poor in this world to be rich in faith and heirs of the kingdom that he has promised to those who love him? Yet you have dishonored the poor. Don't the rich oppress you and drag you into court? Don't they blaspheme the good name that was invoked over you? (vv. 5–7)

James says the rich were excluding and oppressing believers in the world, and yet here there were in the assembly of God's people acting just like the world. In other words, he is saying you are not acting according to the truthful, ancient story—you're acting according to the false narrative of the culture *in God's house*. Instead,

> If you fulfill the royal law prescribed in the Scripture, Love your neighbor as yourself, you are doing well. If, however, you show favoritism, you commit sin and are convicted by the law as transgressors. (vv. 8–9)

Once we are defined by the name of Christ alone, our "isms" cannot fit in God's house and among God's people, lest they try to divide and destroy what Christ has brought together.

They simply are not welcome in His presence. And as we repent of our partialities, we also must smash the idols behind them.

76

ABRAHAM'S SANDS

No one escapes idol-making. We're naturally prone to worship ourselves, and worship tribal gods who look unsurprisingly like us, and who deliver the things we want. Only the power of God can change our hearts to worship the One true and living God and change us to His likeness.

But partiality is not welcome in Wisdom's house. Even in the church, we have trouble resisting our own tribal deities. We self-segregate from others we deem too different from us. Unless our hearts are controlled by true wisdom that unites, we continue to walk past the image of God in our brothers and sisters, smiling wanly at those least like us every time we gather.

Oh, how we love to be judge, jury, and even executioner over one another!

Partiality groups and judges our Christian family by creaturely standards and temporal loyalties. Partiality requires that others conform to my likeness so that my comfort and pride are never challenged. If others cannot think like me, they must agree that my thoughts and actions are playing to God, even when they are not. Conformation to God's likeness doesn't enter the equation.

Partiality is a stench in Christ's nostrils, the incense burned on the altar of a tribal god: a Baal. Why? It goes beyond debasing the image of God in those not like us. Partiality makes a mockery of the covenantal promise itself.

Remember God's covenant promise to Abraham?

Then Abram fell face down and God spoke with him: "As for me, here is my covenant with you: You will become the father of many nations. Your name will no longer be Abram; your name will be Abraham, for I will make you the father of many nations. I will make you extremely fruitful and will make nations and kings come from you. I will confirm my covenant that is between me and you and your future offspring throughout their generations. It is a permanent covenant to be your God and the God of your offspring after you." (Gen. 17:3–7)

The church has a role in the greater scope of this covenant, as the Great Commission springs from it. Inherent here is both mission and commission: blessed to be a blessing to each other, and to the nations; a blessing, not a curse of division and destruction. The church has been marvelously enveloped and ensconced in God's covenant that tears down the idols that drive tribalism, racism, sexism, and even classism, and reconstructs us all as one in Christ.

"I will put my teaching within them and write it on their hearts. I will be their God, and they will be my people. No longer will one teach his neighbor or his brother, saying, 'Know the LORD,' for they will all know me, from the least to the greatest of them"—this is the LORD's declaration. "For I will forgive their iniquity and never again remember their sin." (Jer. 31:33b–34)

God's people were always intended to be marked by Wisdom's unity, not Folly's divisions. Christ's body cannot be torn asunder: from Adam and Eve's first breaths, Christ loves and welcomes all He calls His own.

And so we will always be united, in spite of ourselves.

77

THE HAVES, THE HAVE NOTS, AND THE HAVE SOME MORES

Peter began to speak: "Now I truly understand that God doesn't show favoritism, but in every nation the person who fears him and does what is right is acceptable to him. He sent the message to the Israelites, proclaiming the good news of peace through Jesus Christ—he is Lord of all." (Acts 10:34–36)

Man's partiality is not a part of God's promise to those He calls His own. When we practice partiality, we make false divisions according to temporal categories. We prefer some over others for earthly and external differences. We are moved by our idols. And when our idols tell us what to do and who is our "clique," we are least like Him and most like ourselves.

Yet we forget that at the foot of the cross, we are *all* poor and needy. Desperate need is not just on us, but shot through us. Christ showed no partiality when He entered into the world of Folly. He came into our poverty and sat with us in our deadness. He invited us to His table (marriage supper), dressed us in His clothes of righteousness, bathed us in His love, put us in His house of Wisdom.

> Rich and poor have this in common:
> the LORD makes them all.
> (Prov. 22:2)

From man's perspective, we are a world of haves, have nots, and "have a little bit more than yous." But from Christ's perspective, we all are the sojourner, the fatherless, the widow, the orphan, and the captive made longing for the freedom that only His wisdom can bring.

How then can we turn around and do less? Do worse? The ultimate goal of the kingdom is not to welcome strangers into new social positions, although that's nice. The ultimate goal of the church is to usher them to the table, the home, the fulfillment of the covenant of Abraham. It is only by recognizing our own deep poverty that we are blessed to be a blessing to the nations.

He has not shown partiality in the promise, nor in its fulfillment.

God's mercy triumphs over the judgments we pronounce over others; where we exclude, He includes. Nothing can thwart His mercy.

Note that Scripture sums up the law and the prophets with this: Love your neighbor as yourself, and you will do well (see James 2:8). How are we to love ourselves without worshiping ourselves? We are to think of ourselves with sober estimation, simultaneously knowing who we are apart from Christ, and yet who we are in Him.

In Christ, we realize that we have nothing and everything; nothing of ourselves, and all of Him.

78

FOLLY IS SATAN'S HANDMAIDEN

All who make idols are nothing,
and what they treasure benefits no one.
Their witnesses do not see or know anything,
so they will be put to shame.
Who makes a god or casts a metal image
that benefits no one?
Look, all its worshipers will be put to shame,
and the craftsmen are humans.
They all will assemble and stand;
they all will be startled and put to shame. (Isa. 44:9–11)

Idols always treat us mean and have us singing the blues. Every culture on earth sings some form of "the blues," and it usually rises from
the broken hearts of everyday folk just struggling to make it through life,
the consequences of their own foolish decisions, or suffering under the
cruel hands of others. From country music songs of lowdown love gone
wrong, to the flytings of Iceland, to the plaintive notes pouring from a
Jewish violin, humanity finds a way to express the pain their idols have
brought on them. If you want to hear how idols treat their worshipers,
just listen to how a brilliant blues artist like Etta James howls our pain
and addictive desperation in mid-century blues songs like "I've Gone
Too Far," that names greed as the fuel that continually propels us toward that which only promises to destroy.

From our first indulgence, idols never deliver what they promise.
Then they deliver less and less after that first time, so each time we ask it
to do our bidding their hold on us grows. We naïvely think we've mas-
tered them but it's they who master us. As our dependence on them

rises, their demands on us increase; with each indulgence, they give less and ask even more. True to their alluring, drug-like nature, they work on the principle of diminishing returns.

Folly is Satan's handmaiden. Satan appeals to our greatest craving and need; rather than turning to Wisdom to satisfy and shape us, Folly uses our lusts to satisfy Satan's purposes. Even things that could be blessings and good for us when submitted to Christ can be exploited and become idols if their value and importance are misplaced. And yet we return to them again and again, exchanging Wisdom's truth for Folly's lies, and suffering for it.

With each indulgence our little gods grow in size until they engulf and control us. Our desires become Satan's toeholds, until he rides us like his own two-legged animal with glee and absolute control, his stink of death permeating our hollowed-out core.

Yet until Wisdom steps in, we crave them still. So, if you want to hear how idols treat us mean, go listen to the blues from a woman's perspective. Songstress Etta James lays her voice out and sings our desperation.[1]

And if you want to hear how the church treats God the Father and His Son, listen to "betrayal blues" sung by a man. We can hear the pain of the prophet Hosea echoing in those hurts, and through the prophet we hear God lament and wail over the idolatry of those He loves.

How it pains and angers Him to see us cast His love aside and turn to the cruelty of false gods!

---

1. Etta James (1938–2012) singing "I've Gone Too Far."

79

ENDURING TRIALS
WITH WISDOM

The testing of your faith produces endurance. (James 1:3)

Wisdom instructs us to trust her ways and build our house by training us in the essentials of her circle of knowledge.

Naturally, Folly entices us back to her house by devastating our spirit and capitalizing on our fears; as Wisdom watches, Folly throws a seemingly insurmountable trial in our path that's meant to test and shake our faith. And yet, we may "consider it a great joy, my brothers and sisters, whenever you experience various trials" (v. 2).

Further, we are invited to enter the throne room and make a bold request: "If any of you lacks wisdom, he should ask God—who gives to all generously and ungrudgingly—and it will be given to him" (v. 5). Wisdom bids us to face the trial head-on with an unflinching and resolute steadfastness born by the Holy Spirit.

Despite our fears and quaking knees, wisdom helps us stand firm in the midst of the trial. Finding our resolve demands that we pray: implore God for the discernment to navigate the circumstances, which give way to acquiring newfound *wisdom* about that particular situation . . . and then comes another *test*. It's a circle—a dynamo or a fly-wheel—that produces a kingdom energy and dynamic in the believer's life to accomplish God's purposes, the building of His kingdom through His set-apart people on earth. And the outcome? "Blessed is the one who endures trials, because when he has stood the test he will receive the crown of life that God has promised to those who love him" (v. 12). Still,

No one undergoing a trial should say, "I am being tempted by God," since God is not tempted by evil, and he himself doesn't tempt anyone. But each person is tempted when he is drawn away and enticed by his own evil desire. Then after desire has conceived, it gives birth to sin, and when sin is fully grown, it gives birth to death. (vv. 13–15)

While we are caught here on earth and see things with only partial sight, we may not fully understand why particular trials have come to our doorstep. But Wisdom promises us that one day we will know more and better. We'll see the great ledger sheet of our lives, with its trials and triumphs, losses and gains, perfectly reconciled and balanced by the Great Judge of the universe, and upon seeing we will be satisfied. His economy is redemption, and His law is justice and mercy given in perfect measure. "Every good and perfect gift is from above, coming down from the Father of lights, who does not change like shifting shadows. By his own choice, he gave us birth by the word of truth so that we would be a kind of first fruits of his creatures" (vv. 17–18).

This is Wisdom's eternal mindset.

God will get glory from our trials, just as He brought glory from His own.

Stand fast with joy . . . and see.

80

PERFECTING THE
IMPERFECT

Wisdom's elegant, purpose-filled, and creative fingerprints are over every detail of our lives.

Throughout the Bible and into glory, a soul is not a soul without a body. The body matters, along with all of its specificities, including its timing, ethnicity, culture, and location.

It mattered to Christ quite literally. Old Testament saints knew who the Messiah would be, mostly by physical characteristics and details: born of a virgin, one without sin, a male of Jewish lineage, and so forth. Christ was identified as the long-awaited Messiah, in part, by who He was in body—His gender, ethnicity, and the time and location of birth into a culture within the context of a particular season, according to a divinely appointed guiding star in the nighttime sky. There were no accidents surrounding His entry into our physical world. Every aspect of His arrival had meaning and purpose.

While the Bible tells us Christ was ethnically Jewish, it also tells us that He is the true and perfect human. As Creator and Lord of the nations and the only perfect participant among the nations, Christ identifies with each nation with such completeness, depth, and totality that only He is able to ultimately consummate and bring them into harmony. He gathers the nations to Himself and stands as the perfect African or European; the perfect Asian, Latino, and so on, with all ethnicities, tongues, and tribes. In His flesh, He is the Creator and the perfection of us all.

> After this I looked, and there was a vast multitude from every
> nation, tribe, people, and language, which no one could num-
> ber, standing before the throne and before the Lamb. They were

clothed in white robes with palm branches in their hands. And they cried out in a loud voice:

Salvation belongs to our God,
who is seated on the throne,
and to the Lamb! (Rev. 7:9–10)

He will sit on His throne with great satisfaction at our perfection, and not only to appreciate His handiwork in the details of our bodies. He gives existential meaning to the specifics and wisdom of each of our physical details; and we will realize that it was important that He spoke over us so intimately: you will be woman; you will be male. This one to China, this one to Brazil. He is sovereign and wise even over our historical time and geographic placement. And we have specially assigned work according to each perfect, lovingly assigned detail.

When we embrace His incarnational design as intentional, we embrace Christ's ingathering of all nations, tribes, peoples, and tongues to worship around His glorified body on the throne. In His body, both temporal and glorified, He stands among us and above us as Ultimate Man and Ultimate Ethnic.

Christ is more human . . . and more divine . . . than any of us will ever be.

81

SATAN ISN'T CREATIVE, JUST GREAT AT MARKETING

All things are wearisome, more than anyone can say.
The eye is not satisfied by seeing or the ear filled with hearing.
What has been is what will be,
and what has been done is what will be done;
there is nothing new under the sun.
Can one say about anything, "Look, this is new"?
It has already existed in the ages before us.

ECCLESIASTES 1:8–10

O ur wise and loving Creator has mercifully limited Folly in the amount of destruction she can wreak—both on the earth, and in our individual lives. Satan works in at least three ways to frustrate God's people and hinder them from communing with Him. He works *preternaturally* in the unseen realm; he works *tangibly* through individuals in the visible realm; and he works *systemically* through wicked governments and culture structures.

Satan is incredibly uncreative, unimaginative, and limited in his creativity *because God has limited him.* Folly and destruction might rule this world for a time, but because of God's ultimate and preeminent sovereignty, Satan is limited in his.

Why is Satan so effective at what he does? Satan is uncreative but still very good at marketing; we fall for Folly's repackaged temptations, age after age. He knows what we like, and how to deliver it to us in new and unsuspicious ways.

Satan and God, Folly and Wisdom, are not equal forces. Satan is a preternatural creature *under* God's sovereignty. If Satan and God are equals, then God is not God.

While the societal fabric of oppression may change from age to age, the general contours of Folly's abuse and degradation remain the same. We see the repeat of dehumanizing forces from one oppressive regime to another, from one age to another. These forces include confusion of identity and personhood, violation of personhood, mutilation of bodies and souls, the very questioning of reality as we see it, and the arrogant assumption that we can create alternate realities of our own.

There is nothing new under the sun, including God's sovereignty and restraining, redemptive hand over all.

82

FOLLY'S SCREECH
OF VIOLENCE

The greatest threat to a hostile culture is a massive exodus from Folly's house.

Transformed Christians grate like sandpaper against Folly's status quo. Those who leave Folly's house and become loyal to Wisdom and His Word are presented as a drain on society. We become society's "problem" to those in power, and the loss of souls must be managed by force. Jesus said,

> "Look, I'm sending you out like sheep among wolves. Therefore be as shrewd as serpents and as innocent as doves. Beware of them, because they will hand you over to local courts and flog you in their synagogues. You will even be brought before governors and kings because of me, to bear witness to them and to the Gentiles. But when they hand you over, don't worry about how or what you are to speak. For you will be given what to say at that hour, because it isn't you speaking, but the Spirit of your Father is speaking through you." (Matt. 10:16–20)

Folly looks from her window and counts her losses. She sees people growing and making life after Wisdom's kind, emaciated bodies once starved of spiritual food now growing strong and healthy with a biblical identity. She observes that the once aimless and lazy are finding new purpose; long-held grudges are dissolving under reconciliation and forgiveness. Perhaps this is the worst thing that Folly could see: strength to stand up and publicly call her what she is—foolishness, destruction, death.

"Brother will betray brother to death, and a father his child. Children will rise up against parents and have them put to death. You will be hated by everyone because of my name. But the one who endures to the end will be saved. When they persecute you in one town, flee to another. For truly I tell you, you will not have gone through the towns of Israel before the Son of Man comes. A disciple is not above his teacher, or a slave above his master. It is enough for a disciple to become like his teacher and a slave like his master. If they called the head of the house 'Beelzebul,' how much more the members of his household!" (vv. 21–25)

Folly releases her wolves from their pens to nip at the heels of the newly wise. They bark and nip, bite and scratch, but the train of exodus moves on.

Folly's call becomes a screech in the public square, hurling invective and hate. She will call us every name that she is, in order to stop the hemorrhaging from her ranks.

83

CONFOUNDING THE
NOT-SO-WISE

Wisdom's eternal mindset tells us that all things are working together for good for those who love God and are called according to His purpose, and that it is this purpose in the sweet by-and-by that gives meaning to our trials on this side of the nasty now-and-now.

In the same way the Spirit also helps us in our weakness, because we do not know what to pray for as we should, but the Spirit himself intercedes for us, with inexpressible groanings. And he who searches our hearts knows the mind of the Spirit, because he intercedes for the saints according to the will of God.
We know that all things work together for the good of those who love God, who are called according to his purpose. For those he foreknew he also predestined to be conformed to the image of his Son, so that he would be the firstborn among many brothers and sisters. And those he predestined, he also called; and those he called, he also justified; and those he justified, he also glorified. (Rom. 8:26–30)

However, it's hard to adopt this mindset when the world comes crashing down around us. In moments of crisis, we are told to do the thing that seems most counterintuitive. We're exhorted to pray. Even if we don't know where to begin or what to ask for, the Spirit of God and Wisdom will do the heavy lifting.
Christ's will for us is a will of love. Even in the midst of our pain. Even in the midst of sorrow. Even in the midst of loss that stretches us beyond what we think can bear, Wisdom is there. His redemption of all things makes His will a will of purpose, perfecting, Pentecost, and power.

No death, no resurrection. No resurrection, no Pentecost. No Pentecost, no power. No power, no perseverance. No perseverance, no perfection in glory. All things come from Him, even the perseverance, even the power, even the perfection, and yes . . . even the trial.

Be assured that God does not delight in the trial; He is no masochist, like Folly. He is only pleased in that the trial is useful in establishing His purposes. He does not delight in our terror, our fear, our pain. He did not delight in His own. But He endured for the sake of the eternal mindset.

Whatever it is, God has allowed it for a reason. Let's wait on Him to see what it is.

In underground churches, troubles are "go time." During a massive earthquake in one region that resulted in heavy fatalities, rather than seeking shelter for themselves, two sisters set out to knock on doors to tell their neighbors about Jesus. Those who survived continued to tell others of the kingdom priority, and in this way the church grew out of the rubble. Imagine what trust it takes to think of eternal life before temporal, even as the ground shifts beneath your feet. The eternal mindset sees the kingdom priority in the midst of grave danger. The world calls them "fools," but God smiled on them.

In Wisdom's mind, trials are meant to produce spiritual maturity and kingdom opportunity—but only if we see with Wisdom's eyes.

84

LOSS IS GAIN,
DEATH IS LIFE

In the days, months, and years after the US bombings of Hiroshima and Nagasaki, Christian theologian Kazoh Kitamori began to question God's place in such devastation and physical suffering. No one in Japan—no one in the world—had seen such atomic devastation upon buildings, bodies, souls, and psyches. As the fire smoldered for months beneath concrete and brick, this thought also burnished an imprint of Wisdom and Folly onto his heart:

> God responded to this pain of ours in an astonishing way: he made it serve as testimony to his own pain. God could only reveal his pain to man through our own pain. God uses our pain as testimony to his. . . .
>
> Unbelievers do not recognize their pain as a symbol of the pain of God; the fiercer the pain, the greater their estrangement, to the point of complete separation. But the unbeliever's response to trials . . . to pain . . . becomes a living witness for the unbeliever to the power of redemptive suffering, and in that way to the beauty and redemption of Christ.[1]

Trials drive Wisdom-dwellers to draw closer to Wisdom and the cross; pain pushes Folly-dwellers further away.

Our steadfastness—our holding strong and drawing closer to the only One who understands our pain—is a witness to the gospel. Not only does our pain teach the wise, but it also schools the foolish about the present and future realities of Christ. They will not draw near themselves, so we do it to receive comfort, and so that they can see where our comfort lies.

---

1. Kazoh Kitamori, *Theology of the Pain of God: The First Original Theology of Pain from Japan*, 1st ed. (Richmond, VA: John Knox Press, 1965), 52, 62.

Blessed is the one who endures trials, because when he has stood the test he will receive the crown of life that God has promised to those who love him. (James 1:12)

The crown of eternal life for those who love Him, and also for those who come to love Him, through our surrender to a whole-life witness.

In Wisdom's world, then, trials have life-giving potential: eternal life potential and new life in this life, just as it was for Christ dying and bringing many sons and daughters to glory.

This is wisdom's universal principle that confounds the world: loss is gain. And death is life.

85

THE WISDOM OF
PRESENCE IN TRIALS

"Do you now believe? Indeed, an hour is coming, and has come,
when each of you will be scattered to his own home, and you will
leave me alone. Yet I am not alone, because the Father is with me.
I have told you these things so that in me you may have peace.
You will have suffering in this world. Be courageous! I have
conquered the world." (John 16:31–33)

S olomon Andria is a thoughtful and prolific Madagascar-born African theologian. Dr. Andria reminds us that

living a normal Christian life, especially in the face of temptations,
demands wisdom: That is, the ability to distinguish good from
evil, truth from falsehood, and the important from the useless and
to make timely decisions that conform to what is right. Therefore,
we must ask for it, without doubting the love of God, who always
answers prayer.[1]

Regardless of a believer's circumstance or situation, through discipleship a Christ follower should move from foolishness of an unexam-
ined life to wisdom of a life submitted to Christ; moving from chaos,
rebellion, and destruction to shalom.

This imprint of wisdom on those who dwell with Christ—whether
in the garden pre-rebellion or after the cross in redemption—creates
the byproduct *shalom*. It creates a supernatural peace and patience deep

---

1. Solomon Andria in *Africa Bible Commentary: A One-Volume Commentary Written by 70 African Scholars* (Grand Rapids, MI: Zondervan, 2010), 1536.

within marked by the blessings of *presence, provision,* and *peace,* and is easily recognized by those who have known its inexplicable comfort. Our heads become clear, and we think with new eyes, able to discern wisdom from folly at the precise moment when we need wisdom most.

> The eleven disciples traveled to Galilee, to the mountain where Jesus had directed them. When they saw him, they worshiped, but some doubted. Jesus came near and said to them, "All authority has been given to me in heaven and on earth. Go, therefore, and make disciples of all nations, baptizing them in the name of the Father and of the Son and of the Holy Spirit, teaching them to observe everything I have commanded you. And remember, I am with you always, to the end of the age." (Matt. 28:16–20)

The assurance of deep, Spirit-wrought wisdom that accompanies our most difficult trials and tragedies is one of the ways that Christ is with us to the very end of the age; one of the myriad ways in which He fulfills the promise to never leave us alone.

We grow wise in trials, because we walk more closely with Wisdom when trials come.

86

THE BOOK THAT
MATTERS

The beast was given a mouth to utter boasts and blasphemies. It was allowed to exercise authority for forty-two months. It began to speak blasphemies against God: to blaspheme his name and his dwelling—those who dwell in heaven. And it was permitted to wage war against the saints and to conquer them. It was also given authority over every tribe, people, language, and nation.

All those who live on the earth will worship it, everyone whose name was not written from the foundation of the world in the book of life of the Lamb who was slaughtered. If anyone has ears to hear, let him listen. If anyone is to be taken captive, into captivity he goes. If anyone is to be killed with a sword, with a sword he will be killed. This calls for endurance and faithfulness from the saints. (Rev. 13:5–10)

L ife on earth for the Christian will get ugly. Yet without affliction and hardship, we would be trivial, superficial, flat-sided beings, people without depth or substance, with only a shallow faith; we would be fools yet again.

What principles of endurance can we glean from Scripture's promises in light of the hardships to come?

We can't separate life in the sweet by-and-by and the nasty now-and-now; without one, we can't have the other and so we live for today with hopeful eyes fixed on tomorrow. Some Christians place heavy emphasis on the reality of this world, while others focus unduly on eternity as if present hardships and injustices don't matter. But these who persevere deal in both, and use our future hope to shape our present reality.

Because it's tethered to today, political power is fleeting. The Christian is always one cultural wind away from dwelling in the land of Goshen. No matter how much political clout any group amasses, there will always come a day when a new pharaoh is coming who has no regard for our interests.

Seeking political and cultural power in the nasty now-and-now may see our names in men's and women's history books, but only One will write our names in the Lamb's Book. We will study and marvel over His Book for eternity, and the subject matter between the two is quite different; the victories are recorded very differently, and we are not the hero.

87

CALLED OUT,
SET APART, SAFE

Then Pilate went back into the headquarters, summoned Jesus, and said to him, "Are you the king of the Jews?"

Jesus answered, "Are you asking this on your own, or have others told you about me?"

"I'm not a Jew, am I?" Pilate replied. "Your own nation and the chief priests handed you over to me. What have you done?"

"My kingdom is not of this world," said Jesus. "If my kingdom were of this world, my servants would fight, so that I wouldn't be handed over to the Jews. But as it is, my kingdom is not from here."

"You are a king then?" Pilate asked.

"You say that I'm a king," Jesus replied. "I was born for this, and I have come into the world for this: to testify to the truth. Everyone who is of the truth listens to my voice." (John 18:33–37)

History is long. Sometimes it's so long, we get comfortable; so predictable that we forget not only who we are, but who we are becoming. When we forget the core of our identity, we forget what we are capable of accomplishing. We slip into the sloth of Folly, and plod one day to the next as if we are no different from the world.

We forget that God is sovereign over the houses of Wisdom and Folly, and that He has expected ends for the inhabitants of each. But He is not willing that any should perish and so He waits.

As His waiting becomes ours, perhaps we begin to doubt. Satan has never stopped whispering in our ears, "Did God really say . . . ?" Who are we going to be? With the rise of resentment against the God of the Bible and His teachings and mission, all modern global cultures are forcing us to define exactly who we are, in whose house we dwell—Folly's house with them, or Wisdom's house against them.

There is no salvation in politics or culture. Will we teach our children to see themselves as perpetual victims, be it victims of persecution or victims of oppression? Are we training them to grasp for political and cultural power to accomplish the work of the kingdom that the church alone can do? Or are we teaching our children to see themselves as a called-out, set-apart people, on task and moving with purpose through their Father's world?

The margin is our true heritage, and because God lives with His people on the margins, His power lives there too. As we find ourselves more and more on the margins, He will breathe new life into us. Our dignity, identity, and significance are restored and fulfilled only in Christ.

For His kingdom is not of this world. This life with its history may be short, but Wisdom is long.

We were born for this.

88

THE WISDOM OF
PERSEVERING FAITH

There's a difference between saving faith and operational faith; wisdom grants us both.

Saving faith is the God-given trust that helps us recognize we are living in the world of folly and destruction, that our foolishness is so ingrained that we need Wisdom Himself to rescue us from our own folly. Saving faith is a grace from God that pays the penalty for our sin and moves us from the house of unbelief to the house of belief. It is the power of God that keeps us safe and secure in Wisdom's house, once there.

Persevering faith is also a grace from God, and it is an operational and necessary tool for navigating Folly's world with the eyes, mind, heart, will, and voice of Christ.

Persevering faith is not something you realize you've been granted, until you are standing in the place where you need it.

"And I say to you, anyone who acknowledges me before others, the Son of Man will also acknowledge him before the angels of God, but whoever denies me before others will be denied before the angels of God. Anyone who speaks a word against the Son of Man will be forgiven, but the one who blasphemes against the Holy Spirit will not be forgiven. Whenever they bring you before synagogues and rulers and authorities, don't worry about how you should defend yourselves or what you should say. For the Holy Spirit will teach you at that very hour what must be said." (Luke 12:8–12)

The world of anti-Christian hostility is a world of ever-changing cultural rules. The ground shifts and destabilizes in an effort to throw us off guard. Oftentimes we cannot plan how you will respond. Try though we might to write a script and consider every contingency, we can't always anticipate what the volatile religion of Cain will do or how they will instill fear.

Take courage. Wisdom shows up with persevering faith.

To show forth Christ's wisdom to a hostile culture, sometimes we must speak or act the truth as a part of prophetic confrontation. Sometimes this is the truth unto discomfort, sometimes it is truth unto death.

This is when you need Wisdom's persevering faith. Wisdom tells us what to say, when to say it, and conquers our fear granting strength. It turns our sputtering words into apples of gold in settings of silver. Timely, digestible, full of life, and whole.

Persevering faith is a witness that builds our testimony on earth and in glory.

89

THE COSTLY INTERRUPTION OF DISRUPTIVE SPEECH

S cripture tells us that even as we dwell with Wisdom, we should also ask not only to be wise, but to exercise our wisdom to ourselves, before each other, and in humility to the culture around us.

Asking for wisdom may be one of the most disruptive prayers we can make. When God answers, He does so in overflow terms, and the wisdom stored up in our hearts has no choice but to flow like a torrent, angering and challenging many:

"A good tree doesn't produce bad fruit; on the other hand, a bad tree doesn't produce good fruit. For each tree is known by its own fruit. Figs aren't gathered from thornbushes, or grapes picked from a bramble bush. A good person produces good out of the good stored up in his heart. An evil person produces evil out of the evil stored up in his heart, for his mouth speaks from the overflow of the heart." (Luke 6:43–45)

The prayer for wisdom then, is the disruptive prayer sure to upset the status quo. Our domestic prayers are too tame. They don't challenge the status quo, they preserve it. "Your will be done" is not a disruptive prayer. "Speak through me, Lord, and bring the consequences" is a disruptive prayer.

Wisdom's disruption brings the intrusion of the coming kingdom into our natural world and pries our fingers off the illusion of control we believe we have on the world.

Stephen spoke boldly, with wisdom, and at the perfect time to the right people—with seemingly horrific results.

"You stiff-necked people with uncircumcised hearts and ears! You are always resisting the Holy Spirit. As your ancestors did, you do also. Which of the prophets did your ancestors not persecute? They even killed those who foretold the coming of the Righteous One, whose betrayers and murderers you have now become. You received the law under the direction of angels and yet have not kept it."

When they heard these things, they were enraged and gnashed their teeth at him. Stephen, full of the Holy Spirit, gazed into heaven. He saw the glory of God, and Jesus standing at the right hand of God. He said, "Look, I see the heavens opened and the Son of Man standing at the right hand of God!" They yelled at the top of their voices, covered their ears, and together rushed against him. They dragged him out of the city and began to stone him. And the witnesses laid their garments at the feet of a young man named Saul. (Acts 7:51–58)

Stephen's disruptive speech was the sermon of his life, and he gave his life for it. Wisdom used that moment to begin a series of disruptions in the life of a young and zealous Pharisee named Saul, leading to a radical change in his entire worldview.

In what powerful ways, then, might God use our disruptive prayers for wisdom today?

JESUS, SAVIOR, PILOT ME

"Lord, if it's you," Peter answered him, "command me to come to you on the water."

He said, "Come."

And climbing out of the boat, Peter started walking on the water and came toward Jesus. But when he saw the strength of the wind, he was afraid, and beginning to sink he cried out, "Lord, save me!"

Immediately Jesus reached out his hand, caught hold of him, and said to him, "You of little faith, why did you doubt?"

When they got into the boat, the wind ceased. Then those in the boat worshiped him and said, "Truly you are the Son of God." (Matt. 14:28–33)

Tumultuous seas stand as one of nature's greatest challenges to our body's senses.

The complete loss of equilibrium that seasickness brings makes us question everything we know to be real: what's stable and what's not, what's moving and what's still, what's off-kilter and what's straight. Our eyes don't know where to look, and our stomachs want to jump into our mouths.

When the swells rock the boat, the more experienced sailors and divers tell us to fix our eyes on the horizon. Our minds and bodies need something steady and stable on which to fix in order to stop the confusing messages.

In the natural realm, it's the horizon.

In the spiritual realm, it's Christ.

Just like Peter focused on walking toward Jesus in the Gospels—as long as his eyes were on the steady point, Christ and His purposes—he was more than fine, he was doing the impossible! But eyes off Jesus and on the circumstances, and immediately the instability of doubt showed its force and he sank.

We can rejoice as we pass through the worst storms because it is making us mature and complete. It is teaching us wisdom, creativity, and causing us to grow spiritually; it is teaching us where to look when the circumstances are swirling around us and causing us to lose our equilibrium.

And the principle holds true for a community . . . a community can lose its equilibrium, not just individuals. Fear is catching, like a cold. Doubt spreads from one person to another like a virus, persuading us to look to false gods and idols for security. On a small boat rising and falling on giant, slapping swells, everyone onboard can be as quiet and green as you please as long as no one's stomach surfaces. As soon as one crew member leans over the side, a chain reaction sets off the rest of the crew.

When we share in the same trial communally, we can rejoice in our current trials together, because we are growing wise together, knowing that God is up to something, redeeming a horrible tragedy in a broken world for our good. We remind each other to fix our eyes on the true Horizon, the only One who can steady a crazy-making world full of injustice and hate, cruelty, corruption, and death. Edward Hopper beautifully wrote,

> Jesus, Savior, pilot me,
> Over life's tempestuous sea:
> Unknown waves before me roll,
> Hiding rocks and treach'rous shoal;
> Chart and compass come from Thee—
> Jesus, Savior, pilot me![1]

---

1. Edward Hopper (1816–1888), "Jesus, Savior, Pilot Me," 1871, https://hymnary.org/text/jesus_savior_pilot_me.

91

ABIDING IN
THE VINE

Fresh-picked fruit is a hallmark of bounty. A cluster of grapes cascading from a cornucopia among the vibrant colors of other delec-
tables is eye-catching and promises nutrition.

What the eye cannot see, however, is that once it's nipped from the
vine that fruit has begun to die.

With just the right climate and conditions, that blessed grape cluster can maintain its beauty for thousands of miles as it makes its way
from a faraway farm a half-world away, to a hungry and appreciative little mouth—such is today's commercial produce industry.

Even just to move from the tree to the local market in a basket full
of wares, it can look good for quite some time.

But despite all appearances, once the nippers separate it from its life
force, its decay has begun.

So it is with our disobedience. Unless we abide in Wisdom and remain in the True Vine, there is no life. Jesus' illustration is especially
pertinent.

"Abide in me, and I in you. As the branch cannot bear fruit by
itself, unless it abides in the vine, neither can you, unless you abide
in me.

"I am the vine; you are the branches. Whoever abides in me
and I in him, he it is that bears much fruit, for apart from me you
can do nothing. If anyone does not abide in me he is thrown away
like a branch and withers; and the branches are gathered, thrown
into the fire, and burned.

"If you abide in me, and my words abide in you, ask whatever
you wish, and it will be done for you. By this my Father is glorified,

that you bear much fruit and so prove to be my disciples. As the Father has loved me, so have I loved you. Abide in my love. If you keep my commandments, you will abide in my love, just as I have kept my Father's commandments and abide in his love."
(John 15:4–10 ESV)

It's stunning how good we can appear to outsiders for a very long time, but once disconnected, our spiritual deaths have already begun. We can run about doing ministry, teaching, preaching, and speaking the Word, yet our hearts are far from God and our disobedience has separated us from Wisdom just as it separated our parents from Wisdom in the garden. Disobedience tears us from the tree or the vine, and we die a bit more each day until the rot is undeniable and the damage irreversible, not fit for consumption but filled with odor, mold, and disease.

Our great and wise Vinedresser tells us that nature mirrors life. The way to make life is to have life: to abide with Wisdom in obedience and life, to fall naturally and become a seed for others, and thus the life cycle begins all over again. "No one has greater love than this: to lay down his life for his friends," Jesus assures us. "You are my friends if you do what I command" (John 15:13–14).

92

THE WEIGHT OF
WISDOM

And they compelled a passerby, Simon of Cyrene, who was
coming in from the country, the father of Alexander and Rufus,
to carry his cross. And they brought him to the place called
Golgotha (which means Place of a Skull).

MARK 15:21–22 ᴇꜱᴠ

The beating must have been horrific. His accusers bludgeoned
all strength out of Him with their clubs and their mockery. Eyes
swollen and misted by a veil of blood, the man known for the strength of
His craft had been felled like a mighty oak, straight down to His knees.
Palms flat on the dirt road, droplets of spittle, blood, and sweat dappled
the ground and the backs of His hands. From His hands and knees, He
panted for air amid their taunts and chants. Winded, His breath caught
in unsatisfying gulps, knowing that the most excruciating suffocation
was yet to come.

As the Wisdom of the universe humbled Himself, Wisdom Himself
was being humiliated. Yet in that humiliation, there was still much more
road to walk.

Reluctant Simon, repulsed by the spectacle, was torn from his two
young sons in the crowd and commanded to pick up the heavy beam.
Simon responded to the rough tug of the Roman soldiers—when a Roman guard barked, you moved. The words were sharp and frightening
to the foreigner: "Pick it up. Now!" What a chaotic scene. Simon the
Jew had heard murmurs that this man was innocent. If true, then there
was something horribly off, unjust, about this whole scene.

Simon's hands, shoulder, and face would have rubbed against the
warm, sticky, strong-smelling blood that already covered the cross. How

heavy that cross must have been for them both, but in vastly different ways. Simon lifted hundreds of pounds of fashioned tree trunk—some scholars speculate a cross would have weighed three hundred pounds—difficult to carry, nearly impossible to drag through the streets.

And yet that same cross for Jesus was a far heavier burden—a cross weighed down by thousands of years of His own creation, broken by man; the weight of man's sinful condition. Heaviness, darkness, sorrow, and death.

> "Must Jesus bear the cross alone, and all the world go free?
> No, there's a cross for ev'ry one, and there's a cross for me."[1]

Simon entered into Wisdom's wake, one plodding step at a time.

The reluctant foreigner compels us to remember Wisdom's humiliation, and the unique significance of *His* cross. In his day, many bore crosses of shame through Roman-occupied streets. But Christ's was different.

This cross was Christ's alone to carry.

Though Simon bore it part of the way, only Jesus could carry its *full* weight. Only Jesus, the Loving Innocent, could turn the heavy weight of eternal shame, judgment, and death to a tree of hope and promise.

We are much like Simon. We realized how heavy that cross truly was, and that only Christ could complete its mission. It was *He* who lifted the heavy cross from *our shoulders*! The hope of "three days later" was Simon's and is still ours. Once embraced, we've entered into the fellowship of His sufferings.

---

1. Thomas Shepherd (1665–1739), "Must Jesus Bear the Cross Alone?," 1693, https://hymnary.org/text/must_jesus_bear_the_cross_alone.

93

WHEN THE ETHIOPE
WAS MADE A MAN

Now an angel of the Lord said to Philip, "Rise and go toward the south to the road that goes down from Jerusalem to Gaza." This is a desert place. And he rose and went.

And there was an Ethiopian, a eunuch, a court official of Candace, queen of the Ethiopians, who was in charge of all her treasure. He had come to Jerusalem to worship and was returning, seated in his chariot, and he was reading the prophet Isaiah.

And the Spirit said to Philip, "Go over and join this chariot." So Philip ran to him and heard him reading Isaiah the prophet and asked, "Do you understand what you are reading?"

And he said, "How can I, unless someone guides me?" And he invited Philip to come up and sit with him. (Acts 8:26–31 ESV)

Wisdom drew the man to worship. Known only as "the Eunuch," his disability defined him.

His disability not only defined him, it limited him from his goal for traveling so far. Though not a Jew, he had come to find Wisdom and worship the King of the Jews. He had traveled far, only to be likely refused at the temple door—he was that one thing that could never enter into the holy gates; he was *unclean*.

The pejorative itself was as filthy rags, bringing the muck and mire of the religious culture on him. The religious leaders didn't even know that the promises they guarded in the temple had been fulfilled, or that they too had been set free; if they had known it was so, they would have told him with the joy of Philip who met him in the road.

As it was, his own body testified against him and kept him from entering the temple, made *unclean* by the hands who enslaved him. For him, the temple door was shut and he could not darken its doorstep (see Deut. 22:30–23:1).

A man in Wisdom's eyes, but a piece of a man in Folly's, he was *unclean*. The cry of the leper, the taunt of the crowd:

"Unclean."

"And the eunuch said to Philip, 'About whom, I ask you, does the prophet say this, about himself or about someone else?' Then Philip opened his mouth, and beginning with this Scripture he told him the good news about Jesus" (Acts 8:34–35 ESV).

Cruel hands had crushed, castrated, and cursed his manhood. Yet Philip brought him great news! Folly's destruction was redeemed by the nail-scarred hands of Wisdom the Creator, Wisdom the Savior. His faith had brought him to Wisdom's door, he was welcomed inside, and he was made clean and new.

"'See, here is water! What prevents me from being baptized?' And he commanded the chariot to stop, and they both went down into the water, Philip and the eunuch, and he baptized him. And when they came up out of the water, the Spirit of the Lord carried Philip away, and the eunuch saw him no more, and went on his way rejoicing" (vv. 36–39 ESV).

Thanks be to God for this beautiful African man, made whole, clean, new. Are we any different? We who were foreign are brought near, we who are broken are made whole, and our mutilated souls are redeemed . . . all at Wisdom's healing hand.

94

FIGHTING THE
LORD OF THE FLIES

You prepare a table before me
in the presence of my enemies;
you anoint my head with oil;
my cup overflows.

PSALM 23:5

The sheep bot fly is a parasite that is found all over creation. These flies invade the nasal passages, cavities, and sinuses of domesticated sheep, and their presence is so predictable that good shepherds plan for "fly time." Female flies deposit a droplet containing live larvae on the nose of a sheep. Those larvae travel up the nose and into the sinuses of the unsuspecting sheep, driving them mad with annoyance and rot. Their growth is stunted, their wool thins, and they won't produce milk. In their desperation and ignorance, they butt heads and spread the larvae to other sheep, and a flock is easily ruined.

Ruined, that is, unless the shepherd in his wisdom intervenes on first signs of the bot fly attack.

The enemy, that crafty lord of the flies, has sent Folly on an errand to ruin sheep and, if possible, entire flocks. To stop Folly's destructive work, the tender, wise shepherd prepares an anointing oil—sunflower, cinnamon, olive oils—and applies it to the sheep's head. Holding a stubborn animal's head is a hard proposition, but the wise shepherd presses in with care to stop the invasion. The shepherd has to get intimate and tactile with the sheep if destruction is to be defeated before it works into the brain.

And there he is, face-to-face with his sheep, searching, inspecting, rubbing oil on the nose and the fleece. The oil must feel good to the sheep as it goes on. Parched skin, cracked-sore and dust-dry, made supple again as the ointment quells the movement of the worms. Finally. Peace.

His hand is upon his own, and this is where the healing is—in his hand. In his touch, the cup of healing overflows. Imagine our Great Shepherd, oiling away our anxieties that infiltrate our minds and destroy our confidence and hope; imagine being touched by the very hand that made you in His image.

We are not alone in our anxieties and cares. Surely David, the shepherd boy who knew that King Saul was in hot pursuit to snuff out his life, had his bot flies too. Though he knew about the worries and pressures of life pressing in on mind and body, he also knew only the Wise Shepherd knew the secret to their relief.

Only goodness and faithful love will pursue me
all the days of my life,
and I will dwell in the house of the LORD
as long as I live.
(Ps. 23:6)

95

WISDOM BREATHES
EX NIHILO

"Rejoice, childless one, who did not give birth;
burst into song and shout,
you who have not been in labor!
For the children of the desolate one will be more
than the children of the married woman,"
says the LORD.

ISAIAH 54:1

While Isaiah is speaking directly of the post-exilic community in Judah, he is also speaking more broadly of the future glory of true Israel. In the chapter before, Isaiah paints the future with his prophetic words, revealing the anguished victory of the Suffering Servant, Christ Himself.

Now, the Servant's task is seen as fulfilled and the prophet breaks into a hymn and shouts of praise from the "barren, childless woman," welcoming the dawn of the new age.

Stop. A *barren, childless* woman? Did we read that passage clearly? What reason could a childless woman possibly have to rejoice?

It's ironic that Isaiah uses a childless woman to illustrate Christ's eternal covenant of peace for His bride. In his culture, being childless was a shameful state, yet these were the conditions into which Christ would come. When God spoke through the prophet of a "redeemed barrenness," he spoke directly against Israelite culture. The Israelites had gone beyond glorifying the inherent good and blessing of motherhood to idolizing it as a salvific condition for women. The fruitful ones made the barren woman a scandal in her own hometown, a shameful reproach in her own home.

God's wisdom is not the wisdom of man; His wisdom confounds all expectation. Some of the greatest recorded blessings of God came through barren women; women who were tormented and marginalized by their own culture, even by their own servant-maids. We need look no further than Sarah, Hannah, and Elizabeth; motherhood in each of their cases was an act of God, for God's purposes alone.

Even barren *places* birthed great fulfillment—after all, can anything good come from Nazareth? Yes, and amen! Christ Himself didn't come into Israel at a time of the great kings, or after a great victory in battle; He was born into Israel when there was no fruit on the fig tree; true to the words of Isaiah, He came to Israel after a lengthy silence from God, "like a root out of dry ground" (Isa. 53:2).

In God's economy of redemption, the barren woman receives a double portion: temporal blessing as well as eternal. Sarah became the mother of nations, Hannah nursed the prophet who would anoint a king after God's own heart, and Elizabeth reared the herald of the coming Christ. All provided symbols of supernatural kingdom fruitfulness and expectant hope beyond the temporal into the eternal.

Yet the fruit-bearing in view in Isaiah 54 shows an even greater miracle: fruitfulness in glory is promised from no birth process whatsoever, either natural or supernatural.

This is truly worth noting then, as Wisdom has always specialized in creating *ex nihilo*—in bringing something from absolutely nothing.

Creating something from nothing, good from evil, fruit from rot, is something that Wisdom alone can do.

96

UNCOMMON FAMILIES, UNTIMELY BORN

Enlarge the site of your tent,
and let your tent curtains be stretched out;
do not hold back;
lengthen your ropes,
and drive your pegs deep.

ISAIAH 54:2

Folly is doing her work among families, causing fractures, injustices, and wounds sometimes too deep and dangerous to navigate for the human soul. These deep cracks in God's foundation mean an increase in children growing up in single-parent households, and in many cases it means generations are maturing never knowing "mother" and "father" together in a functional sense.

What does spiritual motherhood and fatherhood mean in such an environment?

It seems that some of us who've never married or borne children will come to fulfillment in parenting somewhat akin to the way that Christ met Paul, as to ones "untimely born."

Paul didn't meet Christ in the natural manner of the apostles, walking alongside Him on the crowded roads during His earthly ministry; yet his comparatively unconventional encounter with the glorified Christ on the dusty road to Damascus held no less value, meaning, or impact than that of the other apostles.

Such is it with spiritual motherhood and fatherhood, when we are "untimely born."

Spiritual parenthood offers an opportunity to become a wise and compassionate influence on our current "social orphans," adults who have been left with a parental void of wise counsel, compassion, or love. When the church steps in to address their spiritual and life issues, she speaks against a long line of opportunists offering an endless supply of false identities to wile away their hours, days, and years.

As spiritual parents, we anticipate Christ in glory as He gathers in the nations under His name alone, the only name by which we are eternally known. We are able to enlarge God's tent and ours far beyond parameters restricted by our own name or blood. By intimately ushering the motherless through the practical and spiritual aspects of life, the "never-married" and the childless all participate in the redemptive kingdom-building process, and foretaste the joy of spreading His tent pegs wide, enlarging His territory, and accomplishing His plans of gathering in His own to His throne.

Children are a memorial, biologically and spiritually. Naturally, we want to see our own familial names continue on after we are gone, but for those of us "untimely born" into spiritual parenting, our desire is far greater to see the name of Christ magnified through subsequent generations.

The question then is whose name will our children memorialize? Our personal name that is temporal and will one day pass away, or the name that is eternal and above all?

97

WISDOM BLESSES SPIRITUAL MOTHERHOOD

For you will spread abroad to the right and to the left,
and your offspring will possess the nations and will people
the desolate cities.

ISAIAH 54:3 ESV

Once one has borne children, one can't know what it is like *not* to
have borne them. Bearing children and not bearing children are
two different existential frames of reference. Of course, the woman who
has borne children can know what it is to mother one not of her own
blood, if not through adoption, then certainly through mentorship.
Conversely, the barren woman may never know the joy of bearing children, yet the joy in view in Isaiah 54 is apparently one that can only be
known *in the absence of natural childbearing.*

Through spiritual motherhood, the barren woman experiences a
cause for praise that the *natural* mother *will never know*, receiving blessing in the temporal and storing up treasure in the eternal.

In God's wisdom economy where things are reconciled very differently from the way the world thinks, the childless woman can recognize
the great kingdom potential that lies within her. Spiritually speaking,
we are all barren apart from the regenerative power of Christ to draw
us to Himself and make us new. Motherhood—indeed parenthood
in *any* form—should be life-changing for all involved as we share joys
and sorrows, disappointments and victories, and find meaning in them
from God's perspective.

Through the influence of older and wiser spiritual mothers in our lives, our questions change from "How does God fit into my childlessness?" to "How does my childlessness fit in with God?" Isaiah 54 moves us beyond wanting comfort for "what has not been," and helps us resist those who treat spiritual motherhood as a mere consolation prize. When we see the nations stream through our front door hungry for "mother" and godly counsel, we realize that even infertility may have a great and exalted impact on the kingdom.

Truly, to be regarded as "mother" when one technically and biologically *is not so* is a simultaneously exquisite and humbling experience. Wisdom has brought a surprising and unspeakable joy that battles Folly's work in our broken world, and that pushes against the darkness that wants to consume us all.

98

EVERY GIFT
TO THE WISE

Christianity will always outlive her pallbearers.
—Vance Havner

Despite the declarations of the demise of the church from the voices of secular enlightenment, she is not dying—she is becoming. Christianity may be changing, but that doesn't mean the church is dying. She is merely ceasing to seek salvation through politics and culture, and becoming what she always has been since God's mercy clothed our parents in the garden, since Abel's costly obedience, and in Christ's ultimate fulfillment of our identity: a beautiful, Spirit-wrought, other-political, other-cultural reality moving through a fallen and hostile world.

We are becoming less American Christians, and more Christians in America, realizing where our temporal identity lies despite the fact that we are so far from our true Home. In this world, none of the wisdom contained in Scripture offers any assurance of political or cultural dominance for the people of God, but only life more abundant through the cross of Christ.

It's popular in our day to overly criticize the church and highlight her failings, yet for every history book written exposing where the church got it all wrong, history is marked with unknown and overlooked saints who, despite their human failings, walked more closely to the New Testament story of the people of God.

These are the stories and the skills and the values and the virtues and the priorities that we will need in the years to come as persevering global Christians . . . just passing through.

If we are not willing to speak the truth of Christ to all powers around us, and if that truth does not include Christ's ability to transform the wicked and redeem histories, then surely our activism and our accounts of history are impotent. Proclaiming truth to a wicked and adulterous generation is to search for Folly's hostages looking to escape her house of bondage—to declare that He is Wisdom, His Way the only way, His Truth the only truth.

> Let no one deceive himself. If anyone among you thinks that he is wise in this age, let him become a fool that he may become wise. For the wisdom of this world is folly with God. For it is written, "He catches the wise in their craftiness," and again, "The Lord knows the thoughts of the wise, that they are futile." So let no one boast in men. For all things are yours, whether Paul or Apollos or Cephas or the world or life or death or the present or the future— all are yours, and you are Christ's, and Christ is God's. (1 Cor. 3:18–23 ESV)

All our stories—through history and in the contemporary world, from among all nations and ethnicities who believe on the name of Jesus Christ—are bound up and rooted in the story of the kingdom of God. This is the ancient story of a people created, set apart, kept, and perfected by a covenant-keeping God. This is the message for which men and women are incarcerated around the world, for which women and men and children around the world die. It is the message on which we stand, and by which we are saved. That love was fully demonstrated through Christ, that while we were yet sinners, He died for us . . . according to the Scriptures.

It's okay to love the church, and to love her back into our true reality. Just as the prophets of old did under Wisdom's command, we use Wisdom's words to call them back to Wisdom's house . . . and in doing so, we love Wisdom Himself.

99

WISDOM TO
STAND

Let love be without hypocrisy. Detest evil; cling to what is good. Love one another deeply as brothers and sisters. Take the lead in honoring one another.

Do not lack diligence in zeal; be fervent in the Spirit; serve the Lord. Rejoice in hope; be patient in affliction; be persistent in prayer. Share with the saints in their needs; pursue hospitality.

Bless those who persecute you; bless and do not curse. Rejoice with those who rejoice; weep with those who weep. Live in harmony with one another. Do not be proud; instead, associate with the humble. Do not be wise in your own estimation.

Do not repay anyone evil for evil. Give careful thought to do what is honorable in everyone's eyes. If possible, as far as it depends on you, live at peace with everyone.

Friends, do not avenge yourselves; instead, leave room for God's wrath, because it is written, Vengeance belongs to me; I will repay, says the Lord. But if your enemy is hungry, feed him. If he is thirsty, give him something to drink. For in so doing you will be heaping fiery coals on his head.

Do not be conquered by evil, but conquer evil with good. (Rom. 12:9–21)

In every age, Wisdom calls us to warm ourselves around her hearth and gather for family talk. We are called to speak honestly about the cultures that surround the people of God wherever they are found. We are likewise called to talk about the communities who call themselves Christian, but still despise the true Christ who transforms people to love God's decrees, His created order, and the call to love those who persecute us.

Folly hates Wisdom's love, because it's the key to their hostages' freedom from Folly and her father the devil. Around Folly's hearth, which has no fire to warm us, sure we can talk about God. One can even talk about a very vague Jesus. But speak of Jesus as Lord over all of your life, the Jesus who transforms, and Folly's teeth begin to gnash.

We are being conditioned to stay silent when the wisdom of Christ makes Folly-dwellers uncomfortable. Secular ideologies condition us to shrink from stretching out our throats and proclaiming the thoroughly transformational power of the gospel of Jesus Christ; they instead want us to replace Him with their pale version of the real thing, where there is no power at all—only an open grave of numb acceptance, where another shovel of compromise throws dirt and shame onto our faces that have turned away from Wisdom Himself.

And where politically progressive Christianity demands that we shrink in silence and politically conservative Christianity says we must dominate, Wisdom calls us to die. The mark of the true Christian is not social or political action; it's death on the cross so that Folly becomes Wisdom, a Cain becomes an Abel, and the church becomes who she was always intended to be: a called out, other-cultural, and other-political reality kept safe by her covenanting and all-powerful God.

The gospel calls us to stand in love for Christ first, and to keep showing up with that love when we are shown the door . . . or summoned to a courtroom . . . or burnt with the hot flame of social ostracization . . . or felt our cheek welt up from the back of someone's hand.

For surely this is what Romans 12 envisions in the grandest of terms. When Paul starts speaking in these verses, there's a simple yet profound theme that echoes throughout the entire New Testament, and even through the whole of Scripture. This is the truth wrought by Christ and refined by persecution:

It's okay to love the church. It's okay to love the outcast. It's okay to love the unbeliever with truth. But we can only love well—and love as they hate—by loving Wisdom—Christ—first.

And it's when we love in the midst of hate that we are most like Him.

100

WISDOM AND HOPE BOUND TOGETHER

"Write to the angel of the church in Philadelphia: Thus says the Holy One, the true one, the one who has the key of David, who opens and no one will close, and who closes and no one opens: I know your works. Look, I have placed before you an open door that no one can close because you have but little power; yet you have kept my word and have not denied my name.

"Note this: I will make those from the synagogue of Satan, who claim to be Jews and are not, but are lying—I will make them come and bow down at your feet, and they will know that I have loved you.

"Because you have kept my command to endure, I will also keep you from the hour of testing that is going to come on the whole world to test those who live on the earth. I am coming soon. Hold on to what you have, so that no one takes your crown.

"The one who conquers I will make a pillar in the temple of my God, and he will never go out again. I will write on him the name of my God and the name of the city of my God—the new Jerusalem, which comes down out of heaven from my God—and my new name.

"Let anyone who has ears to hear listen to what the Spirit says to the churches." (Rev. 3:7–13)

Our Christian ancestors knew they were fighting on the winning side today, *because* of their hope in God's tomorrow. They trusted that in Christ's kingdom, God would wipe every tear from their eyes that had been caused by temporal injustices. They trusted that God would balance the scales between the temporal *and* the eternal worlds.

They understood then what we must never lose sight of today: that hope today and tomorrow are inextricably bound together and cannot be uncoupled.

Since our garden days, God's people have been pressured to declare allegiance to another or themselves. In the midst of these siren calls from earthly social, cultural, and political identities, we pray that we will remember whose we are at our core, the ones who are called by His name, His mark upon our souls.

Yet there are those around us who deride our hope as an empty promise, as mere "pie in the sky." Let us be wary of those in our culture who are determined to mark us with a different name; they attempt with their mark to erase our hope in the eternal, for they are intent on erasing Christ, the root of our hope. We must not unwittingly allow anyone to turn us away from the very person who promises to sustain us against hostility; our faith in things hoped for and unseen is one of the greatest weapons in our storehouse. Folly wants nothing less than to steal our confidence, our eternity, our security, and rob us of our peace—of course, she will scorn our inheritance that was intended for our hope.

Persevering Christians have always known that Christ's kingdom is not limited to this temporal world, and that a better day was coming. Christians always have a duty to protect this eternal hope. The sweet by-and-by is not a psychological pacifier; it is a guarantee that God has sworn by Wisdom Himself to make what is wrong in the nasty now-and-now. Therefore, let us boldly rebuke any who disparage our eternal Hope, and commend our ancestors for their temporal resilience *and* their eyes of faith. By doing any less, we sweep the legs out from under our own perseverance and hope today.

Our ancestors found no shame in the eternal promises of the sweet by-and-by, and neither should we. They used the promises of glory to propel their work in the nasty now-and-now.

Let us then do the same.

EPILOGUE

God proves with each generation through Scripture that He will keep His covenant promises, even when we are foolish and disobedient. However, His covenant keeping does not absolve us of our responsibility to obedience or to the exercise of wisdom according to His Word. At any given time, we are either moving toward life, or we're moving toward death. Paul further qualifies the foundation of these two poles by framing them in Romans 6 as "dead to sin" or "alive in Christ."

We've not been left floating haphazardly in a world of foolishness and chaos. As we anticipate glory, we're told that the Holy Spirit will guide us into all knowledge and truth. The people of God must walk together knowing that in every age, lasting peace is only built on wisdom's foundation.

In our current age of moral relativism, it's imperative that we ground ourselves in truth. As we disciple those God loves, the question "Is this course of action wise?" seems to go hand in hand with questions of right and wrong. Biblical wisdom, when pursued in the community of the local church and applied to all areas of life, has the potential to produce good and reliable Christians and to produce holiness in them. In times of persecution and rising anti-Christian hostility, the choice to follow Christ's ways may lead to destruction of our physical bodies, but such choices based on obedience to His Word that place us in the fellowship of His sufferings will never lead to the destruction of our souls.

In applying redemptive wisdom to life's tricky concerns, we cannot fear sharing our own stories with the people we disciple and interact with and tell them about God redeeming our own foolish and destructive life choices. Because we all know the compelling call of foolishness, we cannot be afraid to risk a relationship to say, "This path is destruction. This path is life." Waiting prayerfully for loved ones to turn from foolishness preserves both our love and our hope.

It seems prudent to bear in mind that many Christians are attempting the decades-long road of discipleship in a microwave-oven world. How much pressure does our own impatience exert when we demand that a new convert show an instant and seemingly perfect desire for a sacrificial life that honors God above all? Yet as we walk alongside with prayer and long-suffering and do not give up, we display our own belief in Wisdom's promise that He who has begun a good work in each of us will faithfully complete that work until the day we are all perfected in His presence.

Because of the creative work of Christ, wisdom and shalom *were* our right in the garden, yet stolen from us by the enemy of shalom.

Because of the redemptive work of Christ and through His obedience, wisdom, shalom, and the peace that passes all understanding is a present right for all who have inclined their hearts to Him as the ultimate source of wisdom. Through the work of the now glorified Christ, we will dwell—this time, undisturbed—in the new heaven and the new earth.

This is the restorative work of wisdom . . . just as it is the redemptive work of Christ.

ACKNOWLEDGMENTS

"First giving honor to God, who is the head of my life . . ." His patience with me is unparalleled.

In my quest to write about God's wisdom, it's taken many people much wiser than I to bring my thoughts to print. As per usual for my personality, I approached the learning curve at 100 mph. These are the people who helped me wisely apply the brakes so that the project could finish well.

My husband first noticed God was answering my prayers for wisdom, mostly in the form of difficult personal circumstances. I'm grateful to him for encouraging me to pen my thoughts and observations as I opened up Proverbs 8 and 9 to quell my anxiety over difficult decisions. "I don't know the answer to this, but God does" has become a staple in our wisdom vocabulary. It's the one phrase that slows down my "fix-it quick" nature and reminds me of my dependence on God who knows all things actual and all things possible.

For more than a decade, precious prayer and Bible study groups at my local fellowship New City Glenwood in Chattanooga, Tennessee, have patiently helped me grow wise through study, example, discipleship, and the friendship of trusted beloveds. Younger men and women have invited me into their lives as a spiritual mom, creating a sweet, wisdom exchange in the midst of a constantly shifting culture. Those who've clung to Christ have given me a front seat to watch wisdom shape them—it's been an honor to love and be loved by you.

Through the years, there have been a handful of women and men who spoke wisdom to me, over me, and into me. Ledonia Kimball, Deena Stuart, Dorothy and Richard Bennett, Grace Odums, Sally and Marvin Mickley, Nancy MacHarness, Nancy DeMoss Wolgemuth,

Emmitt and Janice Cornelius, Thomas Harvey, my professors and colleagues at Reformed Theological and Westminster Seminaries, and many others have all shaped how I approach and apply biblical wisdom today.

Last, I'm grateful for the wise counsel of Don Gates and The Gates Group, Trillia Newbell and my team at Moody Publishers, and Pam Pugh's editing skills—she has polished my thoughts and made them sing. Thanks also to established authors Jasmine Holmes, Jackie Hill Perry, Nancy Guthrie, and Nancy DeMoss Wolgemuth for lending knowledge and encouragement in this new venture called "authorship."

Thanks to you all for inhabiting *Wisdom's Call*.

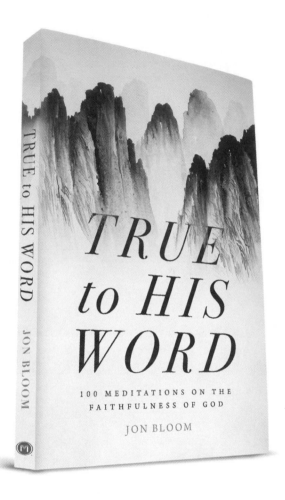